Praise for Looby's first book, *People & Permaculture: Caring and Designing For Ourselves, Each Other and The Planet*

… an outstanding contribution to an ever evolving vision which is creative, imaginative, sustainable and joyful.

Satish Kumar, *Resurgence* magazine

An enlightening handbook for those who want to change the world.

Melissa Corkhill, *The Green Parent* magazine

… grounded, practical and brimming with joy for the good stuff.

Alys Fowler, gardener, writer and presenter

Looby Macnamara's inspiring and groundbreaking book is a rich celebration of the interconnectivity of all life … It is the very best of guidebooks: entertaining, instructive, nurturing and profound.

Glennie Kindred, author and celebrant

Looby Macnamara has been worth waiting for: she fills the bill with luminous clarity, lean eloquence, and an exquisite knowledge of systems.

Joanna Macy, author of *World as Lover, World as Self* and co-author, *Active Hope: How to Face the Mess We're in Without Going Crazy*

… Looby Macnamara uses her solid grounding in permaculture to show that its principles and thinking can help us all be effective and hopeful in an age of change and challenge.

David Holmgren, co-originator of the Permaculture concept

Looby's book is an important step towards our goal of personal, social and ecological well-being.

Andy Goldring, CEO, The Permaculture Association (Britain)

This is a wonderful book, both wise and pragmatic, as imaginative as it is intelligent.

Jay Griffiths, author of *Wild: An Elemental Journey*

7 ways to think differently

embrace potential
respond to life
discover abundance

LOOBY MACNAMARA

Permanent Publications

Published by
Permanent Publications
Hyden House Ltd
The Sustainability Centre
East Meon
Hampshire GU32 1HR
United Kingdom
Tel: 0844 846 846 4824 (local rate UK only)
or   +44 (0)1730 823 311
Fax: 01730 823 322
Email: enquiries@permaculture.co.uk
Web: www.permanentpublications.co.uk

Distributed in the USA by
Chelsea Green Publishing Company, PO Box 428, White River Junction, VT 05001
www.chelseagreen.com

Designed and typeset by Emma Postill

Cover image © Lisa A/Shutterstock

Printed in the UK by Cambrian Printers, Aberystwyth

All paper from FSC certified mixed sources

The Forest Stewardship Council (FSC) is a non-profit
international organisation established to promote the responsible
management of the world's forests. Products carrying the FSC
label are independently certified to assure consumers that they
come from forests that are managed to meet the social, economic
and ecological needs of present and future generations.

British Library Cataloguing-in-Publication Data
A catalogue record for this book is available from the British Library

ISBN 978 1 85623 189 3

Contents

About the Author

Looby has been teaching permaculture since 2002, and is partner of a leading teaching and consultancy partnership, Designed Visions. Looby runs many permaculture and teacher training courses, and a new course based on this book. She has a passion for creative teaching methods and likes inventing participatory activities and games to enhance learning. Her degree in Human Sciences provides a wealth of perspectives to bring into her teaching and writing. She has also trained as a Work That Reconnects facilitator.

She has supported the development and growth of permaculture nationally through her input as trustee of the Permaculture Association (Britain) for 5 years and was Chairperson for the last 2 years. She is still an active member of the permaculture community and is a senior diploma tutor.

She travels to Nepal with her partner Chris Evans to support the Himalayan Permaculture Centre. Looby has founded a fair trade business, Spirals of Abundance, importing organic cotton clothes and other Nepalese handicrafts.

In 2012 she published *People & Permaculture* – the first book to directly translate permaculture principles and design for use in people based systems. Since then she has trained people from all over the world to facilitate people and permaculture courses who have formed the collective Thriving Ways.

Looby enjoys singing, yoga, writing poetry, gardening and making all sorts of things. She lives with her partner Chris and her two daughters, Shanti and Teya. They are in the beginning stages of setting up a permaculture education and demonstration centre in Herefordshire.

For details of her websites see page 122.

Acknowledgements

Writing a book, like most things in life, doesn't happen in isolation, there are many people that have contributed to this, to whom I am truly grateful. I'm thankful for all the multitude of influences that have encouraged me to widen my thinking.

Deep gratitude goes to Chris Johnstone and Jenny Mackewn who skilfully guided me through a Work That Reconnects facilitator development adventure. They really demonstrated how much fun learning can be. Thank you to all my fellow adventurers who shared their experience, enthusiasm and courage. Thank you to Chris and Joanna Macy for their powerful Work That Reconnects intensive at Findhorn in 2013. Much of the wisdom from these courses has flowed into this book.

Thank you to all those who have participated on permaculture courses with me; learning is always two way. In particular thank you to all those from the 2013 People and Permaculture facilitator training who co-created the subtitle with me, and are part of Thriving Ways. Welcome to Angela Embom, Diego Van de Kerre, Demian Burgenik, Denise Curi, Hege Svendsen, Fiona K. O'Neill, Ilse Dupre, Jacqueline Fletcher, Juin Gibson, Kerry Lane, Monika Koncz MacKenzie, Nomalanga, Pauline Lemaire, Peter Cow, Pierre Houben, Wenderlynn Bagnall, who are the coming change makers, bringing in a world where people can embrace potential, respond to life and discover abundance.

Thanks to the teacher training course of 2014 for their input into the last stages of the book; Adam Rogerson, Angie Polkey, Aranya, Dagmara Karbowska, Hafidha Green, Hannah Thorogood, Heidi Hexelltine, Niamhue Robins, Prem Zivkovic, Sarah Spencer, and Simon Carter.

Thanks to the whole team at Permanent Publications for their expertise, support and team work, especially to Maddy Harland for her insights and patience. And thank you to Emma Postill for her work designing the book.

Once again I am grateful to Rebecca Storch for translating my words into beautiful images. Thanks to Fiona O'Neill for her helpful suggestions and edits. Much gratitude to Flora Freemantle, for allowing me to use her home as a writing retreat.

Thank you to my parents for all the thinking skills they have taught me over the years. Thanks to my partner Chris for his on-going love, support, and sharing of ideas. And thanks to my youngest daughter Teya, for her enthusiasm and affection and ways of seeing the world differently. A huge thanks to my eldest daughter Shanti, for proof reading the book and for generally being awesome. I am grateful to live around her unbounded creativity.

This book is dedicated to Paulo Mellett (1979-2014), a warrior of peace; fighting with love, determination, practical skills and a good dose of thinking differently. May his work have many ripples.

Foreword

Over thirty years ago, I went to a talk that changed my life. I was a medical student back then, and had been schooled in a rather mechanical approach to healthcare. That evening I had an 'aha moment', as the ideas of systems thinking were introduced to me in a way that transformed my approach to medicine. Looking back now, I recognise that one of my most important shift points came about as a result of being helped to think differently.

In this wonderful book, Looby Macnamara shines light on more than just one transformational shift in thinking. Ushering in a spirit of abundance, she invites us to explore seven! In doing this, she's breaking away from the idea that there is just one right way to look at or think about things. Instead, she describes how each thinking pathway can take us on a different track.

It is when I'm feeling stuck, defeated or anxious that I gain most from looking at where my thinking is leading me and considering other possible views. When a shift in my thinking opens up a new way forward, it can bring both relief and liberation. Psychologists refer to this ability to try out different perspectives and move between them as 'flexible thinking'. It not only stops us getting stuck in one particular view – research suggests that learning to think more flexibly like this can help reduce our risk of anxiety and depression. It strengthens our capacity for creative problem solving, helping us navigate through the bumps and knocks of life.

Crisis can be a turning point

Whatever challenge we face, whether in our personal lives, family, work, community or world, one thing we have choice over is the perspective we take. If we're feeling stuck, blocked, or uninspired by the options presented, we can try thinking differently and see where that might lead. For example, when facing my concerns about climate change and other disasters unfolding in our world, an idea I find reassuring is that crisis can become a turning point. In the years I worked as an addictions specialist, I saw this many times when clients hit rock bottom and then made their turning towards recovery. When I wonder what I can do to support a larger turning of recovery in our world, I'm glad to reach for the seven ways of thinking Looby describes in the pages ahead.

In Chapter Two she introduces Solutions Thinking, based on the idea that whatever problem you're facing, there is a solution to be found. Is this idea always correct? I don't know. But I remember Edward De Bono, author of Lateral Thinking, writing about two ways to evaluate an idea. One is its 'correctness value', in terms of whether the idea is right or wrong. Another is its 'movement value' in terms of where the idea takes you. One way of thinking about world problems concludes that there's nothing we can do. Thinking like this takes us on a track that leads to feelings of resignation and defeat. Solutions Thinking, by contrast, assumes there is a way and provokes us to actively search it out. A different style of thinking leads to a more energising consequence, with an openness to new perspectives and willingness to experiment.

If planetary crisis became a turning point for positive change, how might that happen? With solutions thinking we contemplate possible pathways, one of these being a cultural shift in the way we think. This book invites you to take part in such a shift, and equips you with cutting edge concepts that can both improve your life and strengthen your capacity to make a difference in the world.

The messenger can also be the medium

In the 1960s, thinking pioneer Marshall McLuhan famously coined the phrase 'The medium is the message'. The way we say something can communicate as much as the words we use. Having known Looby for a few years, I've seen that the way she lives her life communicates the same messages as those you'll find in her writing. She inhabits a mindset that guides her attention and choices in ways that I learn from and find inspiring.

Looby's first book *People & Permaculture* showed how design principles often applied to gardens could also be used to improve our lives and relationships. Inviting us to think differently about permaculture, Looby applies permaculture principles in places they haven't been taken before. In this book, permaculture is one of her sources – but she also draws from other wells, particularly the approach of the Work That Reconnects, an inspiring transformative process first developed by US author/activist Joanna Macy.

One of Looby's favourite quotes is from French author Antoine de Saint-Exupery: "If you want to build a ship, don't drum up people together to collect wood and don't assign them tasks and work, but rather teach them to long for the endless immensity of the sea." Having a vision you long for can fund you with energy, enthusiasm and motivation. But longing is also painful if you don't believe your vision is possible. So as well as longing, you need ways of thinking that help open up a way forward. That is what Looby offers us here, and I'm grateful to her for it.

CHRIS JOHNSTONE
co-author, with Joanna Macy, of *Active Hope:
How to Face the Mess We're in Without Going Crazy*

The thought manifests itself as word;

The word manifests as deed;

The deed develops into habit;

And habit hardens into character.

So watch the thought and its ways with care

And let it spring from love

Born out of concern for all beings.

The Buddha

Introduction

As a child I learnt about green house gases and their effects. I was taught about them in an impassive way – they were just facts, that was what was going to happen, there was no choice in the matter. I remember this niggling doubt, not only about the ozone layer, but about all sorts of things that were happening in the world that seemed to be blatantly bad things – shouldn't people be paying a bit more attention? Shouldn't we be responding more to these problems and trying to change things? There was a question lurking in the background of my mind – what could I do to make a difference?

Fast forward to the 1990s and I was at university. The millennium, which had seemed as far away as the predicted crisis for the ozone layer, was now on the horizon. The above questions were still very present for me but I was no nearer to finding answers. Then permaculture slowly crept into my life. Permaculture is a method of using nature as a guide to design for sustainability. It is a way of thinking that promotes resourcefulness, resilience and creativity. (See page 16 for a fuller explanation.) At first my head didn't really understand the concept, but my senses responded to eating flowers in salads and seeing frogs in simple ponds made from washing up bowls. Friends came back from courses and I sensed a difference in them. They were full of vitality and ideas and were strongly grounded. They were living in an abundant flow of ideas, vegetables, connections, generosity, passion and purpose.

Participating in a permaculture course myself, the ideas took root in my head, heart and hands. I was amongst others who saw problems and were asking themselves what am I going to do? What are we going to do? Where are the solutions? Can we create solutions? And together we were living a strong belief that, *yes* we *can* create solutions. A creative life force was awakened within me. The question – *what can I do to make a difference?* – shifted from the background of my mind to the foreground.

As I connected with other people on similar journeys, I became more aware of the strength of working co-operatively. I felt empowered because it wasn't all just talk, it moved into action; we went from thinking to doing. I found perma-culture to be full of inspiration, magic and common sense.

Permaculture grew in my life, and as I learnt to think like nature I became more sensitive of my own nature, and of myself as a natural system. I also became conscious of the limits for the growth of permaculture. I couldn't understand why earthcare wasn't happening more quickly, if there were so many solutions available to us. I realised that limits are often within us as people, whether it is on an individual level, how we relate to our family, patterns of community living, governmental structures, or inter-national politics. At all levels our dynamics as people can interfere with us looking after each other and the Earth.

I also perceived how much more potential permaculture has for reaching out to people and helping them to live productive, abundant lives. My vision and purpose became about finding ways to make permaculture more accessible and relevant. I wrote *People & Permaculture* to widen the definition of permaculture beyond gardens and farming and translate it for use for anyone and everyone. Since its publication thousands of people globally have benefited from it's processes and structure and have engaged in personal and social designs.

Meanwhile the Work That Reconnects has become a more prominent part of my journey. The Work That Reconnects is set of workshop methods designed to engage us more fully with the world around us, and the consequences of the actions of humanity. (See page 19 for more details on this subject.) It has allowed me to fully embrace my appreciation of the world and myself. I have been invited to lower my numbness bar and open my heart to feel pain for the suffering and destruction I witness in the world. I have felt the continuity of life and expanded into larger timeframes, I have shifted to thinking for the future. I have connected with a deeper source of courage and willingness to speak for a better world and to act on behalf of future generations. Experiential activities have given me ways in which to embody our interconnectedness with all beings, and backed this up with systems theory.

I began this book as a way of answering the question I am most often asked – what is permaculture? There is so much need in the world for inspiration and tools for positive change, and I wanted to find an elegant way to convey the magic, hope and possibilities that permaculture contains. As I reflected upon my journey, I realised it was ways of thinking that had changed and made key differences; they opened up fresh horizons and instigated new behaviours, which have led to exciting outcomes. Changing attitudes of heart and mind have enabled me to feel more secure, positive and proactive. I know there are many people on comparable paths searching for more meaning and purpose. I began to characterise these ways of thinking so that they can open similar doors for others and make real and immediate differences in people's lives.

While permaculture and the Work That Reconnects are different in their methods, I discovered that there are shifts in thinking that are common to both. And indeed there are many other techniques for positive change that fit within these ways. The two approaches have grown together very organically to compose these seven ways to think differently.

The seven ways are; **abundance thinking** – living in gratitude and balance; **solutions thinking** – believing there are solutions to any problem; **systems thinking** – sensing the interconnectedness of all life; **thinking like nature** – discovering nature around us reflected within us; **thinking for the future** – considering larger timeframes; **co-operative thinking** – learning to collaborate with each other; and **from thinking to doing** – moving into action and turning our dreams into reality.

The synergy of permaculture and the Work That Reconnects is potent medicine for a world full of challenges and opportunities. Both offer ways of dramatically shifting the direction humanity is currently taking. The seven ways are all easy to grasp and can bring about significant benefits. They work on many levels from personal to social to ecological to global. Here is my offering to you, a way of simplifying and deepening the profound messages that permaculture and the Work That Reconnects have to offer. These ways to think differently can shift us to a better present as well as a better future.

Permaculture

The overall goal of permaculture is to create harmony with ourselves, between people and with the planet. It is from this greater purpose that all of permaculture theory stems.

Central to permaculture are three ethics: earthcare, people-care and fair shares. The earthcare ethic respects and protects biodiversity of the planet and creates new habitats. Through regeneration and protection of natural resources we are able to improve quality of life for all beings. The peoplecare ethic asks us to care for ourselves and other people and meet our needs in sustainable ways. The fair shares ethic promotes equality, justice and abundance; now and for future generations.

The ethics are quite straightforward and understandable, (though not necessarily followed) and are shared by many worldviews and religions. They provide the 'what' we would like to achieve – then there is the question of 'how' we go about achieving them. With permaculture we approach this question with principles derived from nature, and a methodical design system. There are permaculture principles that serve to deepen our understanding of how nature works, there are other principles that direct us to an attitude we can adopt. These principles can be used to help us proactively engage in whatever situation we are in, and find ways to think differently about it and move us forward. Using the principles we can create resilient, healthy and productive systems. We will explore the principles in relation to each of the ways of thinking in the following chapters, and page 118 has a summary for quick reference.

There are many frequent occurrences in the world that are way outside of these ethics, but they are normalised and we take them for granted. Just following the ethics opens up a bigger picture of possibilities than currently seem achievable. Can we imagine a world where we have peoplecare and no wars, where we have fair shares and no starving people, where we have earthcare and no toxic waste dumps? We need to start believing that these things are feasible in order to bring them into reality.

Permaculture recognises that it is not enough just to be aiming for sustainability. If the ethics were being met already then we could just sustain them, but as there are so many systems being degenerated, we need to proactively work towards regeneration.

Permaculture is a design system that originated in the 1970s as a response to the destruction modern farming practices were having on the environment and economies. It began with a reframing of agricultural strategies and systems, and translating ideas and principles from natural ecosystems into gardens, farms and smallholdings. The different techniques have enabled us to grow our food more productively, and have also opened the door to growing our communities and ourselves more healthily. Through thinking differently we can grow our own lives differently.

Over the last few decades permaculture has evolved beyond the garden and is being used to enhance the quality of life in all aspects. It is being used to improve our health and well-being, our effectiveness in the workplace, communication in our families and groups, and our healthcare and education systems. One of the beauties of permaculture is that we can all use it in unique ways to enhance what we are doing already and to take us in new directions. We don't have to follow a prescribed route of how to use it.

Through replacing paradigms of fear, scarcity and competition with paradigms of trust, abundance and cooperation, we can open our lives to health, resilience and regeneration. Our personal lives can benefit from empowerment, the ability to see solutions and witness and create abundance. Relationships can flourish with stronger connections and co-operative thinking. Society can benefit from holistic thinking and expanding our timeframes to cater for the future. Globally we can provide for all and improve quality and access to basic needs of food, water and shelter. From working against nature we shift to working with nature, in order to protect and restore ecosystems and the fundamental resources of life; soil, water, air and biodiversity.

We move from feelings of disempowerment to accepting responsibility. It can provide a framework for innovative thinkers and anyone wanting change and ready to step up. Instead of considering what we can gain we shift to imagining what we can contribute; we become active creators of abundance. When we look through the lens of responsibility we want to be solutions for the world.

The Work That Reconnects

Joanna Macy and her colleagues first invented this approach and its workshop methods[1] in the 1970s. There is a spiral that we move through that enlivens us and builds our depth of connection. The stages of the spiral are: coming from gratitude; honouring our pain; seeing with new eyes and going forth. We start with reconnecting with our joy, appreciation and gratitude for being alive and all that life has to offer. With this solid foundation we move to honouring and connecting with our fear, sorrow, grief and anger we have for the state of the world, and all the atrocities that have happened. Through this deep reconnection with our feelings of gratitude and pain we are able to access our own truths and responses to the world. This takes us to the next stage of the spiral where we shift our consciousness and see with new eyes the interconnectedness of all life. The last part of the spiral moves us into reconnecting with our ability to make a difference, our skills, direction we want to move forward and where we want to focus our energies.

The spiral works to reconnect us on an experiential level with our feelings about the current and future state of the world. We reconnect with our desire and motivations for change. We reconnect with all of humanity and all of life.

These seven ways of thinking follow a similar pattern to this spiral. We start with abundance and finding gratitude for what we have in life. We move on to solutions thinking where permaculture and the Work That Reconnects complement each other. In the second stage of honouring our pain, we allow ourselves to look directly at the problems and allow our feelings to surface and be voiced. The acknowledgement of feelings about these problems allows us to really engage with our desire and motivation for change. Permaculture then provides a way of engaging with solutions. The next four ways of thinking – systems thinking, thinking like nature, co-operative thinking and thinking for the future – provide us with valuable, differing perspectives and enable us to see with new eyes. The last way, from thinking to doing, matches the last stage of going forth.

Thinking about thinking

We all have maps in our minds; maps for who we are, maps for how the world is. These thinking maps are similar to any map and can determine the routes we take in our lives. Changing the map changes the destination.

The maps we have in our minds are composed of neural pathways, and, as for any landscape, there are some well-beaten paths. Any physical map has a boundary, there may be pages to turn, or the boundary of the paper. This of course isn't where the land ends, there is more that is unseen. The map has a boundary or frame around it. In the same way our thinking maps can have frames around them, even though we are probably oblivious to them, or unaware that there is a way of thinking beyond this.

If you make a circle with your thumb and forefinger and hold that circle in front of you and look through it what do you see?[2] Someone sitting beside you doing the same thing will see something different. If you move your hand closer to your eye you will get a different view, the object that filled the circle before is now less significant, just a detail in a bigger picture. Neither is more 'correct' than the other, just different.

This circle we have just made creates a frame through which we view the world. The frame can determine the scope of what we see, the level of detail, and where we focus our attentions, in the same way that maps with varying scales show us different roads, features and landmarks.

As Emma Kidd[3] describes, "There is more to seeing than meets the eye, as what lies further upstream from 'what' we see in the world, is the cognitive process of 'how' we see the world." The 'how' we view the world is through frames in our mind. We have many frames that are composed of numerous things; including our values, priorities, and purpose. How we view decisions is influenced by all of these things. For example, we may have different priorities from our partner so when an idea is suggested both people see diverse advantages and disadvantages based on their own priorities and may therefore draw different conclusions. The values we have in our lives frame what we see; each family and group has a unique set of values. If one family values creative expression and musical talents while another values a career in medicine there will be different emphasis on how the children spend their time after school. Our values, priorities and purpose are guiding us whether or not they are explicitly stated.

The ethics of permaculture can provide a frame for our decisions, by helping us to choose options that best meet the ethics. This isn't always easy though, for example, it is debatable whether local non-organic food or overseas organic food is closest to meeting the ethics. Local food has a lower carbon footprint because it has less food miles, but there is an environmental cost due to the chemical use, we also don't know about the conditions of the workers, so we can't often assess on the basis of peoplecare. Even without knowing all the facts we can at least begin to ask questions and consider the ethics.

Often there are unsaid cultural norms in our friendship groups, families, schools and workplaces as well as wider societal norms which greatly inform our viewpoints and help to construct our frames without us even being particularly aware of them.

The frames build over time and come not just from our internal landscape but also from the culture we live in. Each person's internal frames influence, and are influenced by, our external behaviours and culture. Our frames are formed from our life experience, and our place in society.

We have temporal frames of reference. How does this work for short, medium and long term? And these terms – short, medium and long – are in themselves subjective and relative. When we ponder the consequences of our actions are we imagining a world in ten years or ten thousand years? Governments are usually viewing things within their electoral cycle time frames of just a few years. Native Americans envisage caring for the seventh generation after us, recognising that our actions have long lasting effects. Even looking 200 years forward to the seventh generation is a minute proportion of the time humans have been on the planet, and a tiny fraction of the time our actions could have ripples for. If we contemplate nuclear waste and the radioactive half-lives of some of its components, such as Iodine-129 with a half-life of more than 15 million years,[4] our current narrow timescapes are dwarfed into insignificance. One of the gifts of the Work That Reconnects is an expansion of our usual timescapes.

As well as temporal frames we have spatial frames. The spatial frame allows us to focus on our immediate surroundings but allows us to block out what we can't see. It permits us to suppose that there are boundaries to the places our influence reaches, it allows us to believe that we can throw our waste to a magical place of 'away', that is outside of our concern.

Comments can be made about the collective, using the term 'we' as if that is a statement of fact, but in fact 'we' is a subjective term and can have many meanings. The 'we' I refer to when I say 'we don't like…' may well be a different 'we' for when you respond 'we do actually like…' One of us may be presuming the 'we' is our family, the other thinking of 'we' as people in the West or 'we' may be used to mean 'we' as humanity, or 'we' as mammals.

Where we view our boundaries to be, affects our decisions and what we consider is the best course of action for the whole. Often we are coming from a human-centric viewpoint and presuming what is best for humanity. What may be best for the planet and other beings is outside the boundaries of our thoughts.

Frames capture things in the moment and sometimes we forget that life resembles a movie more than a photograph. Our frames are often based on our previous experiences of the world and ourselves. We base what we imagine is currently possible on our experience of what has been possible before. We forget that life has moved on and will continue to do so, that circumstances, both internal and external, are dynamic and forever changing, allowing new possibilities to emerge.

These are just some of the frames that each of us views the world through. We have many frames that arise throughout our lives and these reinforce themselves through creating beliefs and patterns in our internal landscapes. Becoming aware of frames through which we see the world is the first step in being able to adapt them for our benefit. These frames serve to reinforce and create the maps we have in our minds. It is important to remember that the map is not the territory; the map is not the land or peoplescape around us.

Shifting our thinking

When we moved our thumb and forefinger circle closer to our eyes we saw different things. We were able to make choices about what we looked at and how close or far away we moved our circle, and therefore the significance of what we saw in our frame. Similarly we are able to make choices about the frames we use.

Sometimes people can get so fixed on their frames that they find it very difficult to see things differently. A lot of us I'm sure have had the experience of trying to give guidance, advice or just another outlook to a friend who is having work or relationship troubles and the other person just seems unable to see this other perspective for themselves.

In seeming contradiction to this our thinking encounters shifts all the time, sometimes with us hardly noticing, sometimes a slow incremental build up to a shift, and other times a change as sudden as a flash of lightning.

> *Consciousness is the most stubborn substance in the cosmos, and the most fluid. It can be rigid as concrete, and it can change in an instant. A song can change it, or a story, or a fragrance wafting by on the wind.*
>
> Starhawk[5]

Changes in our frames allow us to see fresh possibilities and potentials. Suddenly our map of the world can shift from seeing a flat world to a round globe and the opportunity to sail around the planet becomes real in a way previously unimaginable. Our existing maps and frames become outdated, and when they dissolve, other limits may disintegrate with them. We can shift the view we have of ourselves and of what we visualise we are capable of.

Shifts in thinking can occur through books, courses, an activity in a workshop, films, a line of poetry, conversations and so on. Encounters with other cultures through holidays or meeting someone from another country can suddenly make us aware of a different outlook on life. A wildlife programme can open a door into an unfamiliar world of senses and species' dynamics. A turn of phrase from a friend can cause a hairline fracture in our frame. A snippet of conversation overheard on a train can suddenly widen our perspective.

The metaphor of goldfish swimming in a bowl is used in family therapy. The water in the bowl represents the culture we live in, its thinking and behavioural habits, patterns, beliefs and expectations. There are many layers to our culture. Just as we have different microclimates in a landscape, and we can think about weather patterns for a country as a whole, or a region, or a locality, there are also different microclimates of culture – different size goldfish bowls.

Most of the time our culture is invisible to us and we accept it as the way things are, it is only when either we go and look in someone else's goldfish bowl or when someone looks in ours that we become aware of it. I have had friends doing the washing up in my home differently to how I do it, and I am suddenly conscious of how automatically I follow a pattern. Or visiting another country and realising it isn't part of their culture to hold doors open for strangers. Through seeing this I realise that we do it because it is part of our culture in Britain, not an innate human response.

We can have a sudden swing to a new way of thinking or a more slowly brewing modification process. It may be that something provides a turning point but that we can only make the whole shift through acting upon it and practicing it until it becomes embedded.

Each of us has comfort zones of thinking, patterns of thought and well-beaten paths in our minds. And we also have a pattern of reaction to being outside of our comfort

zones; emotions and feelings that accompany us – do we enjoy stretching our thinking and taking our imagination to fresh horizons or does it make us feel awkward to try on a coat of original ideas?

Our thoughts interact with our feelings and go on to produce our behaviour. Shifting frames can alter our identity, feelings, behaviour, friends and allies.

We can make choices about letting go of existing frames and looking for opportunities to redraw new maps, without even being sure of where it will take us or what we will see. We can make conscious efforts to become aware of the frames we are using and seeking new ones. We can open up to novel ideas with an air of intrigue and curiosity.

Landscape of thought

The landscape picture on the opposite page contains seven symbols that can be used to represent the different ways. They can each work by themselves to bring changes, and they can also function synergistically together. In the landscape, they are a single picture and similarly these ways can come together in harmony. Collectively they become a coherent ecosystem or thought system. There isn't a hierarchy of ways, or a logical order to follow; it is more about finding what is appropriate for the situation. They reinforce and enhance each other in non-linear ways. They have distinct parts to play at different times. These ways provide choices in how we think and shift our internal maps. Here is a brief explanation of the symbols to begin our journey.

Abundance thinking – seed head
Nature is an expert in creating abundances. Nature fills every niche, appearing even through cracks in the pavement. When a flower produces seeds it produces many more than

is needed knowing that not all will germinate. Abundances are built-in.

Solutions thinking – path around mountains
Even when problems seem huge, solutions can be found by reframing and rethinking the problems. We can find ways around problems.

Systems thinking – murmuration of starlings
Systems are self-organising. The effect of the murmuration is more beautiful and spectacular because of the synergy created by a huge number of starlings coming together.

Thinking like nature – tree
Trees contain natural patterns that are replicated many times in nature, such as the branching pattern that we see inside of ourselves. The tree is a symbol of longevity. Trees are habitats in themselves, home to many other creatures.

Cooperative thinking – beehive
Bees work together in a host of harmonious roles to keep the beehive functioning optimally. The overall health of the hive is paramount.

Thinking for the future – parent and child
When opening up to thinking for the future we anticipate the consequences of our actions for future generations, both positive and negative.

From thinking to doing – jumping frog
Frogs can be seen as symbols of transformation. As they grow from tadpoles to frogs their whole structure as well as environment and movement change. All of our actions have ripples, and sometimes we just need to take a leap.

The water drop lens

Each of these symbols is contained within a drop of water. Our shifts of thinking are dynamic and can be considered a metaphorical change from a square box to a drop of water, sometimes in incremental shifts, and other times as an immediate switch.

Dr Masaru Emoto[6] has carried out research showing that the shapes of water crystals are affected by words spoken to them. In particular, the words love and gratitude produce stunning crystals. It seems that our thoughts give off vibrations, which water responds to. Our thoughts are literally water vibrating in our brains. Humans are made for the most part from water and this research demonstrates how our whole biology can be influenced by our thoughts.

Water is an ideal metaphor for life, fluidity of thought and transformation. It epitomises the wonder of synergy and emergence. It is something we need to look after for future generations. It is simple and complex, fragile and strong, still and moving. Water can transport and dissolve, cleanse and clarify. Sound and light waves are altered when passed through water. Water can magnify and is a metaphor for seeing beyond the visible. Through a water drop the whole world can appear upside down. Water can be reflective or transparent. These ways to think can be reflected back to our internal landscapes or we can look through to the external. Through water everything on earth is connected.

Why think differently?

Primarily, permaculture and the Work That Reconnects are ways of thinking differently about the world and our place within it.

The question I am most frequently asked is, "What is permaculture?" A less frequently asked question is, "Why use permaculture?" I have looked at where these ways of thinking can take us and illustrated the feelings that can arise and outcomes and benefits we might expect. Our thoughts and feelings are interrelated and both influence our receptivity to life. We can adapt our thinking and change not only the health of our own lives, but the future state of the world.

I have also touched on opposite viewpoints, often the more dominant ways within modern culture, and explored where they might lead us, both on individual and collective levels. It is not always that there is a diametrically opposed mindset, more usually there is a continuum. Sometimes it is simply that there is an absence or lack of this way of thinking.

By using examples from our own lives and from global contexts I have conveyed how interconnected they are, how they need tackling simultaneously and how solutions to both can arise from these ways of thinking. There is a mirroring and echoing of personal, social and global problems, and equally there can be a mirroring and echoing of the solutions that can reinforce themselves and grow. These ways are relevant in our own lives and for the whole direction of humanity and the planet. We cannot underestimate the power of thought. Every physical object, book, film and song was once an idea in someone's mind. The current state of the planet – both our successes and our failures – has arisen through the thoughts and actions of people, past and present.

The seven ways don't need specific training or skills; once we are aware of them we can observe them in our own minds and make choices about how we think. Each chapter of this book ends with a method for bringing these differing mindsets into your everyday life, building awareness and strengthening this way of thinking.

This book serves to open our minds and hearts to new ways of thinking that enable us to thrive in our lives. By expanding our thinking we increase the possibilities available to us.

Embrace, respond, discover

What does it mean to step out of the known and into the unexpected? It can be daunting to move from the familiarity of our comfort zones. There are however wonderful gifts along the way. With thinking differently we enter new ways of interacting with the world. These interactions can be summarised in three words; embrace, respond, discover.

Embrace potential

With open arms, hearts and eyes we are able to embrace what is present for us. We blossom and are able to embrace challenges, surprises, pleasures and opportunities. We see possibilities and gratefully grasp them. We embrace and nurture ourselves, as a parent would embrace a child, giving warmth and attention. We open to the potential within ourselves. And we open to the potential for humanity. There is potential for healing, growth, harmony and peace. There is potential to live in creative, fulfilling and nurturing ways. This openness naturally leads us to respond creatively to life.

Respond to life

Being responsive requires us to be open, engaged and observant. Responsibility is the ability to respond. We can take responsibility for our thoughts, actions, who we are, and how we respond. When we respond to life, we are aware of dynamic, changing, evolving circumstances around us. We can engage with renewal. We pay attention to life – to reality – to what is real and important, to our fundamental needs to survive and thrive. We perceive the need for action and are ready to dive in, use our strengths and enter the flow. We respond to life *with* life. From responding we move to discovering.

Discover abundance

When we look through different frames of thinking we enter into a voyage of discovery. This discovery is a process that unfolds over time. The process is not a passive one, we need to be active with our curiosity and it takes courage to make this journey. From embracing our potential we can access our source of courage. In the same way the surface of water can reflect, what we can discover is our inner abundance; the resourcefulness, resilience and creativity that reside within. We can create fresh routes to abundance, and travel to new horizons. This journey of discovering abundance begins with gratitude. When we welcome and appreciate what is already there we build momentum that allows us to actively create abundances.

With embracing, responding and discovering we are fully alive, we can create positive, resilient, vital and living futures, for ourselves and the whole of life. There are many futures open to us, and we have choice in the direction we move. If we embrace what is there and respond to what comes our way, we will discover what lies beyond and within. Through embracing, responding and discovering we can create a field of thought resonance around the world that is energetic and engaging, inspiring and empowering.

The real voyage of discovery consists not in seeking new lands, but in seeing with new eyes.

Marcel Proust

CHAPTER ONE

Abundance Thinking

Gratitude has a way of turning what we have into enough.
Timber Hawkeye[6]

One of the fundamentals of abundance thinking is the belief that there is enough – enough for us as individuals, enough for us collectively and enough for future generations. We don't need to hoard, be greedy or fearful of sharing because there is enough. There is a security to be found in this belief that is not present if we are thinking in terms of scarcity.

Abundance and appreciation go hand in hand. When we can feel gratitude for what we have and what is around us we open to feelings of satisfaction, awe and harmony. We can celebrate our harvests. We can even celebrate the learning that we gain from our mistakes and congratulate ourselves for the efforts made. We can celebrate what we have done rather than focusing on what we still have left to do. Gratitude starts with appreciation of ourselves.

The frame of gratitude is a potent frame for change. From the viewpoint of gratitude we can feel excitement, resilience, confidence and flow.

Seed head

The symbol of the seed head illustrates nature's way of creating surplus. There are many more seeds produced than is needed for the next generation. Seeds are carried by the wind, animals, birds and water to unexpected places – a reminder that our journey of discovering abundance may also take us to astonishing places.

Within each seed there is potential for a new plant or tree. What metaphorical seeds are we planting in our lives? With the promise of impending growth, we once again can embrace potential.

Real wealth

Gratitude leads us to experiencing our real wealth. There are many forms of abundance we can experience; family, friends, love, opportunities, freedom, peace of mind, well-being, time, creativity, ideas... Ethan Roland[8] identified eight different capitals that compose our real wealth. **Financial** and **material** capitals are most commonly thought of, and include investments, buildings and infrastructure. **Living** capital is in the form of healthy soil, plants, trees and seeds around us. When we have access to these we can grow from good foundations. We can nourish the soil so it can provide further nourishment for us. **Social** capital is the connections we have with our friends and networks. The more we can nurture the connections the more resilience we have. **Experiential** capital is gained through carrying out projects and activities. **Intellectual** capital is found through knowledge and ideas. **Spiritual** capital is expressed differently with varying religions and worldviews; it is based on the idea of developing our spirituality through prayer and worship. **Cultural** capital can only be held by a group of people. It is the shared processes and cultural events such as songs, celebrations and stories.

There is another capital that I wish to add to this, **health and well-being** capital. Our reserves of happiness, joy and enthusiasm for life are contained in this capital. We can see evidence of this when we see two people doing the same job but they have two different outlooks on it, or two people who have the same illness but their different attitudes, which can be based on their reserves of well-being, produce different outcomes.

We all have these different capitals in our lives; they are dynamic stores and can be added to or depleted. The amount of real wealth we feel we have depends on what value is placed on each of these. For example, most advertising focuses on financial and material capitals and ignores most of the others. The skill of the advertiser is to make us feel a lack, and believe that their product can fill the gap. There are cultural differences with what is valued. For instance, many traditional and majority world cultures place great value on social, cultural and spiritual capitals, while these have been eroded in the West due to an overemphasis on financial and material gains.

One of the principles of permaculture is *observe and interact*, how we observe affects what we see, if we observe with an attitude of gratitude and abundance we will be able to see more of our real wealth and be enriched by it.

Inner abundance

Within each of us is a store of skills, talents, purpose, passion, energy and enthusiasm. The lens of abundance thinking is most influential when we use it first to reflect our internal landscape to shed light on our inner abundance. When we are in touch with our inner resources we are more able to see clearly the abundances around us. It is through internal discovery that we are able to make the greatest changes and unearth the most valuable gems.

As Anais Nin believed, "We don't see things as they are, we see them as we are." When a child is full of creativity and wonder they are able to play anywhere with anything; when a child has a belief of 'there isn't enough', then no amount of toys can fill the void of boredom. The same applies to adults; it is through acknowledging and celebrating ourselves that we find a fulfilling world around us.

Abundance and balance

The fair share ethic invites us to live within limits so that resources can be provided for every person and habitats protected for other species. This may seem in contradiction with abundance, but it is inviting us to live in balance; to live within our own and nature's limits thereby achieving balance and harmony in our lives. We can reframe and revalue what we have, in terms of our needs and wants. To live within these limits does not mean to exclude luxury, beauty and quality from our lives; we can find the meeting place between luxury, beauty and quality, and simplicity and sustainability, such as beautiful flowers from our own garden, creating opportunities for us to be in abundance.

There are different ebbs and flows of resources and aligning with natural limits – both our own and nature's – means to tune into these ebbs and flows. We can appreciate whatever is flowing in the moment, and make use of that flow. When there is an ebb we can avoid complaining. Eating seasonally is one way of becoming more aligned with nature's flows. The permaculture principle of *catch and store energy* reminds us to store and have contingencies for the ebbs. Rainwater harvesting is a good example of this. We can capture seeds of ideas when they arise, ready to sprout at a later date.

When water is not allowed to flow freely it can stagnate, so too can we, if we do not allow movement of ideas, knowledge and material possessions.

Acceptance of these ebbs and flows includes managing our expectations, and being content when there is a different outcome. We often get what we need although not necessarily what we want or expect.

Abundance isn't about wanting everything or being greedy or extravagant, it encompasses us thinking about other people and the Earth. We may have to widen our frames and our value systems to accommodate more than just ourselves. The fair shares ethic includes equality of opportunity and voice for everyone in the world. Within this wider frame we are able to see what we have and what we need more clearly.

We are often fed the idea that living within limits involves sacrifices and hardship. However, living within limits has benefits, for example we are fortunate that there are limits on how much we can eat, this avoids us becoming unhealthy and overweight. And ignoring limits has consequences and disadvantages even if not immediately visible. We can choose to voluntarily live within limits that are to the benefit of everyone, rather than limits or rationing being forced upon us in the future, due to decline of resources.

Creating abundances

On our journey to regeneration we will be actively creating surpluses. The permaculture principle of *obtain a yield* reminds us of the importance of gaining from our activities. We can broaden our definition of yield to include enjoyment, friendships, play and so on. These can all contribute to our real wealth.

The fair shares ethic overlaps with earthcare and people-care, the surpluses we create can be reinvested into one of these ethics. In the garden we can provide for other creatures, in our communities we can share our yields.

There is a lot of waste on the planet; time, energy, water, soil, misused communication, food waste, and packaging and on it goes. The principle of *produce no waste* challenges us to stop this, or at least slow it down. One of the shifts we experience is the reframing of waste as resources. Rather than waste being a pollutant it can be part of another system and be of use. So instead of food waste going in the bin it can become compost, water can be used for irrigation, rubbish we see around us can be used to make something else. We can reduce wastage of time by focusing our energies and becoming more effective.

What we name something is important. As well as reframing waste into resources we can also reframe our lacks into abundances. Dry spells have an abundance of sun, downpours have an abundance of water, alone times have an abundance of solitude, and busy social times have an abundance of people. Even a lack of certainty in the future could be reframed as an abundance of open doors and potential pathways. All of these are just flows that will once again shift and change, so we need to capture the moment, be thankful for it and be accepting of the reality of the situation.

Nature is an expert in creating abundances. Nature has a multitude of truths and answers for every situation. As Dewitt Jones[9] describes in his film *Celebrate What's Right with the World*, "When I go into the forest to take photos, nature doesn't say to me, 'There is one great photo hidden here and one photographer will find it and the rest of you will be hopeless losers,' nature says, 'How many rolls do you have? I will fill them all with layers of beauty and possibility beyond anything you've ever imagined, right down to my tiniest seed.'"

When a flower produces seeds it produces many more than is needed knowing that not all will germinate. Abundance is built in. We too can build abundance into our activities.

Sharing allows us to participate in the flow of energy, we can open up to letting go and giving and also open up to receiving. To fully participate in sharing we have to be willing to receive as well as give. There can be an excitement and readiness to dive into the fluidity of energy flow that is present in the universe when we trust that energy will return to us in the form that we need it to.

We can identify what abundances we would enjoy having in our lives and figure out ways of bringing them in. We can use the various forms of capital we have to create wealth in other areas. For instance, we can use our social capital and networks to create opportunities for us to build our experiential capital.

Opposite thinking

The scarcity mindset has the opposing underlying message of 'there is not enough'. The emphasis on lacks, which the advertisers are so cunning at making us feel, extends beyond just our material possessions. The same thinking can be turned inward to ourselves with the message of 'I'm not enough', and focuses us on the things that we can't do, what we don't say, who we don't know and so on. When we look at other people our frames can be filled with their lacks, faults and inadequacies. The world can feel a very unsafe place with no reassurance of providing for us.

When we think about making a difference in the world, if we are beset with feelings of lack we will lose motivation to try. We will be thinking why bother when anything I or we do will not be enough.

One of the tricks of advertising is to confuse us with what we want and what they are offering, to join these up and promise us that their product will satisfy this need in us. The car will satisfy our need for love, the chocolate bar can satiate our need for comfort. This can divert our attention away from the deeper longings of life; the search for understanding ourselves and life, the search for answers to the questions of who we are and why we are here, the longing for connection and purpose in our lives. These cavernous thirsts cannot be fed by food, drink or material possessions. The ignoring of these longings can leave us depressed and bewildered, without understanding their true nature.

The belief that our self worth and status are dependent on our financial and material possessions coupled with the message that what we have is never enough is crippling to our confidence. Inhabiting a scarcity mindset can leave us feeling insecure, paranoid, worthless, yearning and scared for the future.

I hear stories repeated around my friends and colleagues; stories that centre around lack of time and money. It is easy to get caught up in that story as well, focusing on lack of time, money and energy, and to think that what I can and am doing in my life isn't 'enough'. Sometimes it can take a conscious effort to change gears to what is present rather than what isn't available.

There are of course many people in the world that have genuine lacks to basic needs of water, food and shelter. Another outcome of the scarcity mindset is a numbing to these real needs of others. We can somehow block out the pain and injustice of this because we are too caught up with feeling deprived ourselves, rather than focusing attention on providing for them. The scarcity mindset drives the current greed and imbalances of wealth globally. Most of the problems with these lacks aren't derived from there being not enough to go around; food shortages are more often resulting from poverty, distribution and problems of flow. Mountains of food accumulate while people in the same country are starving.

One of the outcomes of not aligning to natural limits is the chasing of energies that involve us putting more in than we get out. If we think of a fox chasing a rabbit it wouldn't make sense for it to expend more energy in the chase then it would gain in food. However, as so many of our systems are subsidised and dependent on fossil fuels we have these sorts of situations around us in aplenty. Some researchers suggest that it can take 10 calories of energy or more (including fossil fuels for chemical fertilisers and transport costs) to produce one calorie of food.[10] The tar sands are another example of a lot of energy being put in to get not so much out.[11] And this isn't even taking into account the full cost of pollution and land destruction. If we use tar sands as a source of oil, the full cost is multiplied as producing a barrel of tar sands oil creates three to four times more climate pollution than producing conventional crude oil.

Benefits of abundance thinking

When we can embrace abundance thinking we can be more present in the flow of life, more empowered, resilient and accepting. When we are thinking in terms of plenty and enough for everyone and other species, there can be longer lasting justice, equality and fairness than if limits are imposed. We can come into alignment with the natural limits and ebbs and flows, peaks and troughs and are able to respond accordingly without fear or greed, bringing a sense of freedom.

Instead of the consumer culture leading us to want more and more, we can appreciate that less can be more. We move from focusing on quantity to focusing on quality. As Satish Kumar says, "Have less food, but delicious, high quality food, then you will feel more satisfied and you will be healthier. Have fewer clothes, but beautifully made clothes and you will be more comfortable. Have a smaller house, but let it be well-crafted and personalised, and you will feel more at home."[12]

Collectively abundance thinking can lead us to a fairer distribution of resources. Ultimately, instead of wars over resources, there could be more open and honest communication in negotiations about how needs can be met and resources distributed. There can be more peace and harmony globally when instead of fighting over resources we can co-operate to conserve and create them.

Discovering abundance

Gratitude is at the heart of abundance thinking. When you notice yourself complaining try and pause and ask yourself, 'What can I appreciate here, in myself, in others and the surroundings?'

Complaining is a cultural phenomena. There are unsaid understandings about when we can complain, to whom and about what. Complaining is a learnt behaviour and therefore can be unlearnt and replaced with something more life enhancing. This can be true of our close relationships when, instead of complaining, we start to appreciate the other person for what they bring to the relationship and begin to nurture those positive aspects. When there is genuinely something we want to improve we can start to focus on solutions to get there.

SHIFTS IN THINKING

Quantity	>	*Quality*
Lacks	>	*Abundances*
Dissatisfaction	>	*Acceptance and appreciation*
Scarcity of resources	>	*Flows of resources*
Domination and greed	>	*Equality, co-operation and sharing*
Priority emphasis on money and financial profit	>	*Valuing real wealth and different capitals*

CHAPTER TWO

Solutions Thinking

When you change the way you look at things,
the things you look at will change.
Max Planck[13]

The primary thing that we need for solutions thinking is the belief that there **is** a solution. If we are lacking the belief then even when presented with possible answers we will be blind and deaf to them. Without the belief it is the same as when we offer a friend advice after advice but they are too caught in the problem for any answer to fit.

With the belief that there is a solution to any problem, we will take the necessary steps to find it. Whatever the problem or dilemma we are faced with, whether it is a personal challenge of losing our job or a global crisis such as climate change, there are ways forward or ways around it or ways to reduce the effects.

Path around the mountains

Problems can often seem to us to be huge, resembling mountains overshadowing our lives. We can change whether we are looking at the mountain or path, the problem or solution. With paths winding their way around mountains we are not able to see their destination, in the same way solutions may be out of our sight and we need to start our journey trusting that it will lead us to the other side. We can travel on paths in both directions. Mountain paths zigzag their way up and down, sometimes solutions can be found by moving in a counterintuitive direction.

Three stories for our time

When we observe the current state of the world there are many problems that our descendants and us will have to face. Problems left over from previous generations, ones that are developing as we speak and ones that will arise in the future. We don't know what the future will bring us; it is dependant in part on what our current actions and thinking are.

From where we are now the state of the world could stay the same, get worse or improve. Joanna Macy[14] talks of three stories of our time to describe these differing outcomes. The first – *Business as Usual* – is where we can carry on as normal. The premise of this story is that there is no need for change and no need to worry about the future. We can carry on with economic growth, global trade, pollution, habitat destruction, etc. and we don't need to concern ourselves with the consequences. It is the story that is often favoured by politicians and the media. Although we are led to believe it can carry on as it is, this is denying the truth of the matter that it can and will change. There are natural limits that are being overridden; we live on a finite planet.

The second story is *the Great Unravelling*. This story is not a pretty one, in this story the true ramifications of our actions are felt and amplified. The fabric of social systems and ecosystems begins to fray and ultimately descends into complete collapse.

There is a third story – *the Great Turning*. The story of *the Great Turning* is one of hope, responsibility and action. Through holding actions against activities that are damaging the earth, through creating alternatives and other solutions and through shifts in consciousness we can find our way to a better world. There is another possible future, full of peace, grace, beauty and care, which we can turn our gaze towards, filling our frame with promising solutions. Our actions can help us step forward in this direction. We can turn away from making more trouble and start envisioning the world we want. The world *the Great Turning* points us towards is a life-sustaining culture for all. Many of us hold the vision that we can come together to create this positive future.

These stories are being played out simultaneously and we can find evidence of each depending on where we look. What appears as isolated stories in the media may actually be parts of a bigger story of *the Great Unravelling*, such as freak weather conditions and emergencies. It may be that pockets of our existing structures can remain unchanged; our schools for example may be able to continue as they are. The small combined actions of groups around the world working for positive change may be the swelling of *the Great Turning*. A lot of time could be spent arguing about which story is true or which story will win out in the end. But we can choose which story we would relish happening. And we can choose which story to believe is possible and where we choose to focus our attentions. This doesn't mean that we don't acknowledge the problems and honour the pain, anger and sorrow they cause. This awareness of the problems is necessary for us to provide the stimulus for finding solutions.

Active Hope involves identifying the outcomes we hope for and then playing an active role in bringing them about. We don't wait until we are sure of success. We don't limit our choices to the outcomes that seem most likely. Instead, we focus on what we truly, deeply long for, and then we proceed to take determined steps in that direction.

Joanna Macy and Chris Johnstone[15]

In *The Fifth Sacred Thing* by Starhawk we enter a future world where both the best and worst possible outcomes for civilisation are manifest. (I imagine also there would be pockets of the world remaining mostly unchanged.)

When we look at life through the lens of *the Great Turning* we are choosing to believe that solutions are possible and that we can find them. We are choosing to hope for the best outcomes and to put our life force behind actions that might bring them into being.

For a lot of people this focus on finding and creating solutions is the key thing that attracts them to permaculture. In a world where we are faced with a lot of problems, from the past, present ones and challenges looming in the future, it can be reassuring to focus on finding solutions.

How can we ... create a society that lives within limits necessary to avoid tipping over into a runaway climate change? This is an opportunity to shift our direction to one built on foundations of social fairness, well-being and happiness, entrepreneurship, the vitality of local economies, resilience, sustainability and inclusion. The reason we step forward and roll our sleeves up and do this is because we care about our families, about others, and about the face of the world around us. And we care about ourselves.

Rob Hopkins[16]

There are many challenges facing us in the world today. Some are experienced by individuals, others affect our immediate villages, towns and cities. Many are being felt most directly by ecosystems. Some of these problems are due to actions of the past, and some problems we will be leaving for future generations. The solutions to these problems will need to arise on different levels as well. Solutions in one arena will bring direct and indirect benefits in another. So while we are fixing things in our own lives we are helping the bigger whole, and when we are helping on social, global and environmental issues we are contributing to our own health.

This global revolution will require a huge shift in thinking to move us away from the build up of problems and to avert forthcoming ones. Luckily there are a multitude of different perspectives, models and approaches to draw upon for creating change and thinking differently. Each one has its own merits and distinctions, and particular applications.

We can be thankful for the many people globally working for social change, environmental sanity, human rights and personal development. Together they are bringing a global revolution, together they are creating *the Great Turning* towards a life sustaining culture. What they have in common is the regeneration of cultures, communities and land through shifting mindsets, creating change and providing alternatives.

Finding solutions in real time

Permaculture can be seen as a way of finding solutions in real time. *Finding* means being proactive in our thinking, doing, reframing, questioning and imagining. *Solutions* move us closer to any or all of the three ethics of permaculture: earthcare, peoplecare and fair shares. There are problems all around us on different scales, and we need to be aware of them. The Work That Reconnects provides exercises that allow us to be honest about all the things that are happening in the world that are outside of these ethics, and engage with our feelings about them. Sometimes it's small stuff that needs attending to, all the way up to really big global issues. Instead of becoming stuck on there only being one way to meet our needs we can be resourceful, thereby building resilience. Within solutions it also means protecting the solutions that are already there, i.e. ways in which the ethics are already being met. *Real time* refers to all three aspects of time: responding to the present moment while maintaining a continuity of time; dealing with the outputs of past actions; and becoming aware of the ramifications of our actions in the future. It also means finding solutions that are appropriate within the environmental and cultural context, not just assuming that a solution in one place will work in another. Permaculture is a process of manifesting solutions and growing the ethics in our lives and the world.

Different types of solutions

For each of the challenges we face solutions can come from different directions. We can have technological solutions, it may be new tools – social or practical that assist us. It may be that we improve ways of communicating – and I don't mean faster Internet or mobiles, but ways in which we can talk and respond to each other in nurturing and kind ways. Solutions arise through movement; home, job, exercise – when something moves, change is instigated around it. Solutions arise from reframing or rethinking the problem.

Permaculture offers many practical solutions to regenerating and conserving ecosystems, growing food and reducing energy use. Water management techniques are used to conserve, harvest, reduce consumption and increase the water holding capacity of soil.

When we look at possible solutions we are generally looking within a certain timescale, both for the work we need to put into creating the solution and for the timing in which we could expect to gain any yields and benefits. For example, planting trees provides many long-term benefits and we may not even be around to harvest from them. There is a dynamic tension between the two permaculture principles of *use small and slow solutions* and *obtain a yield*. On one hand, small and slow solutions can bring us lasting change, provide for our future and allow us to compensate for unexpected changes and tweak our plans as we go along. On the other hand, obtaining short-term yields for our efforts provides nourishment, motivation and momentum. Ideally we want to satisfy both of these.

Thinking outside the box

It's a commonly used phrase, and we are often encouraged to think outside the box to expand our creativity, but let's take a moment to consider the box itself. The box is suggestive of our frame of the world; it defines what we see and understand of the problems as well as what solutions we can see, and it rarely, if ever, will show us the entirety of either.

As Einstein observed, you can't solve a problem at the same level of consciousness that created it. The context and frames of thinking that created the problem need to shift in order to find a solution.

The box is defined by rules, cultural norms, assumptions and beliefs. As we have seen, the belief that there isn't a solution will close our view to solutions altogether. Rules can constrict us, if we don't think it is possible to move goalposts. Assumptions can lead us up dead ends, or close off potential trains of thought. And together they box us in.

Our imagination may have boundaries, based on past experiences of ourselves and of other people that hold us within our own frames of reference.

The privileges we have influence our priorities. For people who have easy access to safe drinking water it is less of a priority to work out how to filter river water and harvest rainwater. These privileges take the problem out of our sight. As the saying goes, 'Necessity is the mother of all invention', but the flip side is that if it isn't necessary to us we are less interested in birthing a solution.

Friends have different boxes and so can help with different perspectives. We are more likely to listen to advice when we are aware of the frames that someone is looking through. If we believe that someone has the answer we are more likely to pay attention. For example, when we want some legal advice we will listen more to a qualified lawyer, who answers within the frame of rules.

There is also a place for thinking inside the box. Sometimes the best solutions are the most obvious, straightforward and sensible. When we have the motivation to look for solutions sometimes they are right under our nose.

Creating win win solutions

We can expand the concept of win win[17] beyond just two people. When looking for solutions we can include other people, the Earth and ourselves. We can try and create solutions where all three ethics of earthcare, peoplecare and fair shares are met.

In nature the edge between ecosystems is a fertile, productive place because it has influences and species from ecosystems on either side. When we try and find solutions that are in the place of winning for all sides, we can find the edge that can bring them together. This doesn't just mean compromising, although perhaps there will be some of that. There can be some letting go and some letting come. Through combining new influences in this edge space, something unique and meaningful is created.

The problem is the solution

The problem is the solution is one of the principles of permaculture that engages us with shifting attitudes in order to find solutions. When we are faced with a problem we look carefully to distinguish its defining characteristics. We then look at these characteristics and see how they might be used to our advantage, rather than expending our energy trying to change them. This principle works well with abundance thinking as it challenges us to appreciate what we have and to put it to use. Within each challenge is an opportunity. For example when our plans change, we can find benefit in our new circumstances. Satish Kumar[18] talks about when he is a pilgrim and has a day where there is no food, he sees it as an opportunity to fast. Here he is thinking abundantly and adapting to ebbs and flows, he is also thinking of solutions and finding the solution within the problem.

We can connect the dots between problems and find that the problem is the solution to another problem, as we saw when waste from one system was used in another.

I use this principle often, especially when I feel disappointed when something isn't as I had anticipated, or if I'm feeling challenged by a situation. This can be small examples of forgetting my wellies when going camping and then having to embrace the opportunity to walk barefoot on the land, or when my emails went haywire and I had to accept and learn to appreciate a few days without them, even though it was at a particularly busy time.

Creativity

The permaculture principle *creatively use and respond to change* is a reminder that change is inevitable and our problems do not exist in a vacuum but in a changing context. This changing context can reveal solutions that were not previously available. Water travels and moves through a landscape, ever changing. It is through being observant and responsive to life that we can dance with challenges that present themselves allowing us to turn them into opportunities.

When I start a creative project I tend to only have a blurry vision of the finished item. I prefer to start somewhere and then be open to following it where it wants to go. We may need to start implementing a solution without being sure of where it is going to take us, because just by beginning both the problem and context will change and we can respond to these changes to find the next step to take.

We don't need to be limited by only one or two possibilities; there may be more than one alternative, just as nature has a diversity of answers to the question of survival.

Using metaphors can be a valuable way of looking beyond the surface and seeing the hidden structure. We can use the patterns from other activities to explore a problem and search for solutions. For example when I am thinking about my poly income (my income from several different sources) I was initially focused on the metaphor of juggling. Not being able to juggle I realised that the metaphor I was using was not helping me to view the benefits of what I was doing and all I was thinking about was dropping balls. So I switched metaphors to something I enjoyed. Firstly I tried a cooking metaphor. I saw how different activities took varying times to prepare and then to 'cook'. How some things can be prepared in advance, some left on the back burner, and some things need to be taken off the heat occasionally.

This helped me recognise the need for preparation and maximising the use of time in between activities, and not letting things burn by having too much going on. It reminded me that part of abundance thinking is giving thanks, and enjoying the meal is a vital part of the process.

I also tried a gardening metaphor to gain insights. Here I saw the benefit of having a healthy soil for any plant to grow in, this led me to prioritising self-care to build my energy for everything I did. I saw that here too there are different timings and growth rates. Linked with abundance thinking I recognised the importance of harvesting yields from my efforts and celebrating them. In the garden, nutrients from one plant can feed another, in my work life, my teaching contributes to my writing and vice versa, increasing the productivity and effectiveness of both. There are many connections between the different things I do and instead of seeing them as isolated parts they came together in a vision of one garden as I explored this metaphor.

Opposite thinking

If we are not thinking of solutions then we are problem thinking. We can either become very intent on the problem or we can ignore it or deny its existence. When we become too focused on the problem instead of searching for a solution, we can feel hopeless, pessimistic and depressed. We can feel trapped inside the problem; anxious and frustrated seeing no way out, yet at the same time dismissive of any solutions offered. It can be very disempowering to be overly focused on problems. Hypochondria is an example of becoming over preoccupied with problems and imagining them into being. For some people it is as if they have a worry box in their mind that needs to be filled at all times.

When we are being driven by the problem we are reactive

to their symptoms and we can end up creating more side effects, escalating into more problems. This pattern is very much seen with pharmaceuticals, where one pill necessitates the need for another. This is contrasted with proactively trying to find and deal with root causes.

The other alternative here is to not be thinking of the problem at all. This happens a lot, the problems of other people and other countries are out of our sight and out of mind. It may be that our privileges mask the problem for us; we don't need to think about how to feed the world because we are being fed, for example. It may be that there is a blissful ignorance around this in part. But another part of us becomes numb to the pain of others, and perhaps guilt, shame and sorrow are background features of our internal landscape knowing that there are many problems unfaced.

Globally there is a collective denial and hence lack of response to the problems faced. This means we may be losing valuable time and problems are getting worse and more difficult to fix. Denial of problems means we are not able to fix them while they are still small and more manageable, as the proverb 'A stitch in time saves nine' reminds us.

Benefits of solutions thinking

When we have a frame of finding solutions as our default position, whenever we encounter problems we can be creative, optimistic, realistic and proactive. We feel more empowered, enthusiastic, confident and resilient because we awaken ourselves to the challenge.

We become resourceful, not taking what we have for granted but using it carefully and wisely in new, innovative ways.

Instead of looking at a situation and wondering what we stand to gain from it, we look to see what we can contribute. Instead of finding blame we take responsibility that leads us into action. We shift from 'I can't' to 'I can' or perhaps together, 'we can'. Together we can tackle the bigger challenges that humanity is currently presented with.

> *The hole in the ozone layer is a kind of skywriting. At first it seemed to spell out our continuing complacency before a witch's brew of deadly perils. But perhaps it really tells of a newfound talent to work together to protect the global environment.*
>
> Carl Sagan[19]

Embracing potential

Looking for solutions requires us to think expansively about the best possible outcomes. The permaculture principle *yield is limited only by the imagination and information of the designer* reminds us that there are always opportunities to enhance what we have and leads us to finding improvements through our creativity and research. We are able to expand, enhance, develop, grow and evolve. We can make incremental improvements to our quality of life and well-being.

Take some time to reflect on the different aspects of your life, asking yourself what is working well, and what is challenging? Then spend time dreaming big and imagining the best possible life for yourself. Bring those dreams into your present life by considering one small step or a tweak to what you are already doing, which will move you forward on the journey to your best possible self.

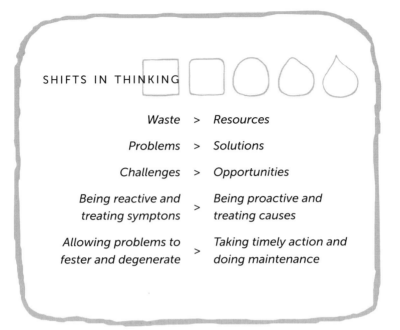

SHIFTS IN THINKING

Waste	>	*Resources*
Problems	>	*Solutions*
Challenges	>	*Opportunities*
Being reactive and treating symptons	>	*Being proactive and treating causes*
Allowing problems to fester and degenerate	>	*Taking timely action and doing maintenance*

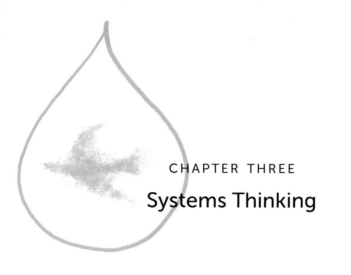

CHAPTER THREE

Systems Thinking

The entire ocean is affected by a pebble.
Blaise Pascal

To think in terms of systems requires a shift from examining individual parts to thinking in wholes. We move from thinking about what things are made of to exploring what they are part of, and what connections and relationships they have. Systems occur at all levels from cells to organisations, from animal herds to transportation. A system is a collection of objects or living beings that are connected and serve a purpose.

Murmuration of starlings

Huge flocks of starlings come together in murmurations, flying together in swirling tornados of beating wings. They are not following a single leader, there is no choreographer directing them. They are a self-organising system, forever changing. Each bird is responsive to what is happening in the flock as a whole. Each murmuration is unique with different individuals, places and formations. They are simultaneously unique and following similar patterns with each one recognisably a murmuration.

Everything is connected

Systems are nested within other systems, reminiscent of Russian dolls, each one whole in itself and held within another whole. Systems are woven together like threads of a story bringing characters together over generations and continents.

Each of us is part of many systems: our homes, extended families, workplace, town, country and our human family. And ultimately we are all part of the entire system that is Earth, which in turn is part of the solar system and universe. Each system is whole in itself but with connections and influences with other systems. Social networks online mimic natural human systems, with overlapping groups and networks, connection points, and the ability to be part of many groups.

Water drops move from one part of the hydrological system to another. A single drop is whole in itself and part of the ocean. Water moves from sky to soil to rivers to sea into the sky again. All water on the planet is connected including water inside of us.

"The tears I shed yesterday have become rain."[20] I first read this line of poetry from Thich Naht Hanh on an umbrella in Findhorn. The previous day I had participated in a truth mandala activity[21] with over a hundred people from around the globe expressing their sorrow, anger and fear that arise from what they witness and have experienced in the world. Feeling empathy for the suffering of fellow people and other beings is a universal human trait, because we know there are connections with all life. This empathy is only absent through numbing and denial, which are learnt behaviours rather than natural responses. The moment of reading these words, in the rain after all the tears, gave me a profound realisation of the connectedness of all life through time as well as space.

Taking a moment before eating to thank all that has come together to create this meal, allows us to recognise the interconnected forces that contributed to it. When we open ourselves to seeing that everything is connected, we open up to extending our care to all beings, to understanding that the Earth is our one home that we all share. Accompanying this there can be a deeper sense of belonging and working together.

Synergy and emergence

Imagine an empty room, there is nothing there and no movement. When one person enters the room the chance of movement or something happening increases. Now another person enters – what happens? What could happen? A conversation is sparked, interaction occurs which can lead to unexpected places. Then more people enter and the number of interactions and conversations increases and soon we have a party!

When we have two or more people there is an energy and creativity that wasn't present with just one person, and there can be unforeseen outcomes. What has just been described is **synergy**. When things come into contact and there is an interaction, an extra energy is created. It is more than just two people standing in the room in isolation. Synergy can be summarised by 'the sum of the whole is greater than the sum of the parts' – for example 1+1=3. We have each part, **and** the relationship between them. When looking after children it can sometimes be more work when we have two because we have needs from both children and the dynamic between them to attend to.

Emergence is when something completely different arises from the interaction that has properties neither thing possesses. Water is a perfect example of this, with entirely different characteristics from either Oxygen or Hydrogen, and unusual properties such as ice floating. Instead of getting 1+1=3 we might get 1+1 equalling a letter, or something never experienced before, such as a quaggle (before you go searching for a dictionary I made this word up).

A friend of mine dislikes egg mayonnaise. He happily eats eggs and mayonnaise separately but put them together and they have emergent properties that he really doesn't enjoy. We can witness this in groups as well; two people that are fine to be around and work with separately are explosive and ineffective when they come together.

Beneficial relationships

Fundamental to systems thinking is the recognition that elements or variables, whether they are people or gases, have an influence on each other. If we go back to our room full of people for a party we see that every person is capable of influencing any other person. Conversations don't need to come through the host of the party. Each conversation, every interaction has a mutual influence.

We move from assuming structures are hierarchical and controlled from the top down, into awareness of non-hierarchical, self-organising systems. Any assumptions we might have had about being in control of everything fall apart when we take into account exchanges and influence. This is broadened to challenging the belief that humans are above the rest of life, replacing it with an appreciation that we are part of the web of life, extending across species and through time.

The number of relationships present increases exponentially with the number of elements. For example when we got two cats we had an additional nine relationships in our household, (there is a relationship between the two cats as well as one between each of the four of us and each cat, and luckily all are harmonious).

We can actively bring things together to encourage exchanges and create conditions for emergence to occur, this is summed up in the permaculture principle *integrate rather than segregate.*

Instead of putting our attention on separate ingredients, permaculture design attempts to understand and nurture relationships between them. It is through interconnectedness that we can maximise productivity and energy efficiency.

Systems at a party

Returning again to the party metaphor we can learn about how a bigger system contains smaller systems. The party, and everyone there, is one big system. Within this though there will be other systems, some are connected through function, some through relationship and others through location.

There might be a kitchen team who are working together for the purpose of providing a meal, with some people chopping vegetables, some cooking, some washing up, others still part of the same system in a different room preparing the table. It is a common purpose that connects all of these people.

There will also be many systems present where people are connected by existing relationships; e.g. a circle of friends, work colleagues, people who travelled together. There will be relationships formed at the party – people who have common interests and are introduced to each other. It is obvious here how one person can be a part of many systems if they know lots of people there.

In one room of the party there may be dancing and everyone in that room is connected by being in the same place. People can come and go and enter or leave that system, but the room itself contains the system and people are influenced by others in that space. Even when we leave the room there may still be ripples of our influence remaining – a dance move that we started for example.

Each of us is in more than one system at any time. Each system is a whole and part of a bigger whole simultaneously. Arthur Kestler coined the term *holon*, from the Greek word – 'whole' with the suffix 'part of'.

Each system has its own pace, timing and rhythm. This can be influenced by other systems. For instance, the children are a system themselves and they could come and request food early, resulting in the kitchen crew speeding up to meet the children's needs. And sometimes there can be a time delay or a gap between systems. At one of my parties, the musicians went to get ready and the dancers followed immediately, not realising they needed time to prepare, an illustration of two systems having different paces and timings.

You can never have the same party twice. Each party and each system has its own behaviours dependant on a vast array of factors. One definition of stress could be trying to predict systems. Like trying to predict a party – who would interact with who, what connections would be made, what connections are already present, what conversations would occur, what jokes and new lingo might arise? A definition of boredom might be a party you could predict.

Each of us will have a reaction to this unpredictability, with emotional and practical responses. Perhaps we think it is not worth trying. Although we cannot predict exact outcomes we are still able to set intentions and define purposes for systems. In doing this we are able to direct energy and focus without tying ourselves to specifics. We can set up a kitchen team without needing to know the exact recipes of what they are cooking.

Each system is self-organising and responds to changes within itself, and adapts accordingly. The dancers pick up on the energy and moves of each other; the music carries people, the music shifts with the flow of dancers. All of this happens without someone in charge directing energy.

Flow versus stuff

The dominant scientific worldview has, for many centuries, been studying what the world is made of. Individual parts are analysed and taken apart to see what they are made of, what happens in between is not noticed or attended to. This is taken forward to viewing ourselves as separate entities. Another school of thought has arisen where we move to thinking in systems and we recognise the flows between parts. We consider what happens in between parts and relationships.

There are many things that could be flowing through someone at any one time; water, food, air, sound, light, hormones, adrenaline, excitement, gratitude, fear, joy, love, ideas, inspiration, conversations, grief, intention and so on. We have choices about how we respond to these flows and, as Joanna Macy says, our choices and actions act as rudders in the flow. When asked to step up to a project or to speak our truth or to act for the greater good in any way, we may have both courage and fear flowing through us simultaneously, but we can choose which one we attend to and which flow to follow. If we choose to follow our courage then this flow will become stronger, even while fear is still present.

When we are aware of ourselves as flow, we can loosen the static picture of our self-identity. We are changing entities that are reactive and proactive to flows around us. We are not the same as a firmly shaped, static block of concrete, we are more characteristic of a candle flame – ever changing, responding to air flows.

We receive information and influences from each system we are a part of. We can use this thought to develop our compassion for others. Whatever they say or do in any given moment has been influenced by the systems they are a part of. When someone snaps at something or reacts in a negative way it may well be more due to the flows of other systems then what has just happened. Instead of casting blame we can move to compassion. Any perpetrator whether it is a small act of annoyance or a serious crime is reacting to influences from larger systems, both in their present and past. Instead of blame when we think of soldiers killing people, we can share empathy for them responding to the system they are a part of. When we think of men abusing women, we can recognise that they are part of a system that teaches young boys not to express their feelings. Of course this isn't to find excuses, as there are always choices that can be made about what flows to respond to. And being this understanding isn't an easy thing to do, monks can spend decades meditating in caves to build up this kind of compassion, but we can at least see this as a possible reaction to aspire to.

When we experience grief, shock, pain, anger, tiredness, happiness or animation we may be responding to a flow from around us. This may be a flow of excitement or irritability in our groups or families. We can firstly perceive this as a flow within us, rather than needing to label ourselves; for example instead of 'I am angry' or 'I am an angry person', we could say or think 'I feel anger arising'. When we feel anger or sadness we may be responding to flows from wider systems, such as being empathetic and feeling sorrow for someone's loss on the other side of the world.

Feedback loops

Each system is responsive to feedback. The process of feedback begins with a receptor monitoring a situation, feedback is then given by the receptor, who then asks for a change to the system, and then a response happens. For example, someone finds the music too loud and asks for the music to be quieter, and then the volume is turned down. Feedback is going on all the time on different scales: Within our bodies, between family members and between nations.

There are reinforcing feedback loops; where the more we do something > the more something else happens > the more we do something. The picture is constantly escalating – until there comes a point of peaking, crashing or popping in some way. This can be observed with children often, where excitement and energy grows and grows, until a crash comes – often pre-empted with the phrase 'it will end in tears'. Reinforcing feedback governs childbirth where the peak is birth.

The other type of feedback is self-regulating. In the same way a thermostat works, the feedback is bringing us back to a reference point or range of activity. Our bodies are filled with these feedback loops that help to regulate our bodily functions, such as temperature.

Sometimes feedback works in opposite ways to what we expect, we may be trying to increase a certain behaviour and instead a decrease happens. Such as when we nag someone to do something and instead of that increasing the chances of it being done the opposite happens and it's less likely to happen. Or trying to untangle a knot and we only succeed in making it more tangled. This is why we need a loop of feedback, so we can observe the effects and adapt our feedback accordingly.

Ways to intervene in a system

We naturally want to affect systems that we are a part of. This is true on many levels, from a parent wanting to improve the dynamic between their children, to governments introducing new laws. But, as Donella Meadows explains, "We can't control systems or figure them out. But we can dance with them."[22] To dance with them, you need to get the beat of the system – to understand the flows and influences, timing and cycles.

In my daughter's school a new head of department started immediately making changes without spending any time observing how the school worked. Although these adaptations such as splitting genders in maths classes had good results in previous schools, they caused a certain amount of chaos and bad feelings in this school. This illustrates the need for getting to know a system before trying to change it. Had time been spent getting to know the school as an individual and unique system, she may have made different choices, or at least introduced it in a different way.

One of the mistakes we make when we try and bring about changes, is that we don't focus on what's relevant. If we are looking at our health or a family dynamic for example, it is our tendency to ring fence around the issue and only look at factors within this. Everything is connected though, and we don't know if what we are looking at is a relevant factor. It may be something that is seemingly unrelated that is the key influencing factor. Perhaps the heating comes on in the middle of the night, disturbing sleep of one of your children who is then grumpy in the morning, affecting family dynamics.

A common way to try and intervene is by increasing what we are already doing. The UK government is proposing that we have longer school hours. This won't necessarily have the desired impact of improving education. Having more school won't make those that don't enjoy it learn any more. Donella Meadows[23] describes doing more of the same as one of the least effective ways to intervene in a system. One of the most effective ways is to shift the thinking. Taking the school example, this could mean engaging the students more in what they are learning and helping them to see the benefits. There could be radical approaches to this, such as school is voluntary, so instead of children going to school because they have to, they need to find their own motivation for being there.

Another example of trying to intervene by changing mindsets is the current surge on trying to shift the attitudes that lead to violence against women. Through trying to shift the paradigm of how women are portrayed in media, the intention is to reduce the number of violent incidents.

Permaculture design seeks to redirect systems that are degenerative into ones that are regenerative. The design process focuses on observation and using the principles to direct change to create healthy, vibrant systems that are beneficial for all their individuals.

Opposite thinking

Reductionist thinking has been the dominant scientific philosophy, leading us to study individual parts and what things are made of. It disregards connections and interactions between parts. When this viewpoint is present in our lives it breeds feelings of separation and isolation. We can feel disconnected and dispassionate about the plight of others.

If we believe the worldview that there are humans on one hand and resources for humans on the other hand, we are stripped of compassion for other species and the land we live on.

When we view the world as separate entities with people and nations as isolated individuals then it makes sense to protect ourselves and maintain our boundaries. When we do this though, we are less receptive to feedback: we don't want to be vulnerable, so we build defences. Defences can be made with money, weapons, isolation, beliefs and closing our eyes and ears. Energy and resources are spent busily maintaining and creating boundaries and borders. This is particularly obvious with nations funnelling huge amounts of money into the military. We become characteristic of a knight in armour cushioning ourselves against blows and viewing the world through a tiny slit. With these defences, we mask feedback from the consequences of our actions. When we wear thick-soled boots we lose contact with the ground beneath us. When we can't feel feedback then we can't respond accordingly.

The reductionist way of reasoning has been used to mask and confuse evidence, and avoid changes. For example, when trying to find the source of hive collapse syndrome in bees over the last few years, many factors have been suspected as relevant. Stress, pollution, disturbance, habitat, poisons etc. are all possibly playing their part rather than one single issue being entirely responsible. This has led to advocates of neonicotinoids[24] (a chemical commonly used on crops) refuting that this is a major cause and hence trying to avoid restriction by claiming it hasn't been 'scientifically proven'.

More than 30 separate scientific studies found a link between the neonicotinoids,[25] which attack insects' nerve systems, and falling bee numbers. Despite these studies the

British government argued that the science was incomplete and said the ban could impact food production. The incompleteness arises from multiple causes. However, the good news for bees is that Europe did vote to ban these chemicals.[26]

We can see this same scenario being repeated where because one thing cannot be entirely the cause it is used as an excuse to not change anything.

The whole story of business as usual is maintained, by ignoring feedback and seeing incidents as isolated, rather than part of a bigger pattern. Everything, including the problems we face are interconnected. When we see newspaper headlines each day as part of a bigger story, the idea that we can just carry on as normal starts to crumble.

Benefits of systems thinking

Recognising ourselves as part of systems that influence other systems and that each system on the planet is connected, we can change from thinking that what I do doesn't matter, to realising that our actions have consequences and are meaningful. Many of the ripples of our actions are beyond our awareness.

Systems act through their parts, as in starling murmurations, each bird is contributing to the whole system. Each small action we take is part of a bigger story, *we* are part of a bigger story. Whenever we do something or act in a certain way we can ask ourselves what is it a part of? What am I part of? What flow am I contributing to?

We can recognise the futileness of trying to predict and control and open up to flow and synergy. Rather than wanting to control outcomes we can accept and embrace emergence. It can be both relieving and challenging to accept that we cannot regulate any system.

We don't know where the tipping points are with climate change. We don't know what disasters might emerge from the combined effects of all the stresses we are placing on ecosystems. Equally though, we don't know the tipping points for Earth recovery. We don't know how our actions when combined together can bring about positive change. The words *emergency* and *emergence* have the same Latin root 'emergere' meaning to arise out of; so perhaps the emergencies we face will give rise to opportunities for emergence.

As individuals there are limits to how much we can achieve, there can be a trap of thinking *I can't*. With emergence we can shift this to the potential of working together and *we can*.

Responding to life

In any permaculture design the first step is observation. Through observation we are able to, as Donella Meadows said, 'get the beat of the system'. In your own life start with identifying what systems you are a part of such as different activity, family and cultural groups you belong to. Then move to observing the flows, relationships, timing and pace of the different systems. Don't try and change anything initially, just observe. After a while, think about how different timings would affect the system, i.e. what would happen if something happened more or less frequently? For example, if you are taking an exercise class once a fortnight you might conclude that you would get better results if it was more often, but equally it may be that if you tried to do it more frequently it might become unmanageable and not happen at all.

Different things are appropriate at different times, and it is through being observant and responsive that we get the most sustained results.

SHIFTS IN THINKING

Stuff	>	*Flow*
I can't	>	*We can*
Predictability	>	*Emergence*
Humans as above everything	>	*Humans as part of the web of life*
Problems seperate	>	*Problems and solutions are linked*
We are too small to make a difference	>	*Our actions have ripples*
Seperate and isolated	>	*Wholes, connections and continuity*
Defending boundaries	>	*Seeing a world without borders*

CHAPTER FOUR

Thinking Like Nature

We are part of a brilliant planet, surrounded by genius.
Janine Benyus[27]

This chapter is central in the seven ways and is really the heart of permaculture. The frames we are using here require us to be open to learning from nature. Ironically, this way would have been natural and intuitive to us in past times, but we have been taught differently and need to unlearn some of that. The premise here is that we are part of nature and we are natural beings, and we have natural processes and connections between us. Nature's rich diversity provides us with bountiful opportunities to expand our thinking beyond our human constraints.

The frame of thinking like nature grows from solid foundations of respect for the Earth. And from understanding nature, our respect grows and deepens characteristic of roots extending into the Earth herself.

Tree

The tree is used here as a symbol for thinking like nature. It symbolises strength and longevity. A tree is composed of many patterns; branching, spirals, concentric circles, all of which are found repeated many times in nature and within our bodies. Trees are whole ecosystems in themselves, providing habitats for many creatures. We can learn to be rooted while still being flexible. The potential of an acorn to grow into a majestic oak tree is a reminder of the enormous potential contained within each of us.

Earthcare ethic

The Earth is a living organism, able to self regulate, evolve and sustain the multitude of life upon it. Life has been undergoing a period of research and development for a few billion years. What is present on Earth is a result of organisms finding ways to adapt to their environment, this is the genius that Janine Benyus talks of.

Respect for the complexity and diversity of life, treasuring ecosystems and caring for the land around us are at the core of the earthcare ethic. We move to a place of valuing all life for its intrinsic worth.

Patterns in nature

Nature is composed of repeating patterns; repeating in cells, plant leaves, even galaxies. We can feel a kinship with other species when we recognise the same patterns running through our veins as through the channels of a tree.

Our windpipe branches into bronchioles and then into the alveoli of our lungs just as the trunk of a tree turns into branches and twigs. This same branching pattern carries us from motorways to main roads to country lanes.

Our inner ear carries sound through its spiral shape just as a whirlpool concentrates energy flows and a corkscrew burrows down, creating the force needed.

We can watch our heartbeat on a machine resembling waves of the sea. The disks of our vertebrae show rings typical of the trunk of a tree. The pores of our skin interlock in the same way as scales of a pinecone. The structure of our bones, a tightly woven thicket akin to a bird's nest.

Each pattern in our body can be seen in nature time and again, with different sizes, colours and textures. Nature has reasons for these patterns, they provide an efficient way of exchanging energy or nutrients, keeping warm, using space, protecting, catching and strengthening.

Nature follows patterns in time as well as physical patterns: daily, seasonal and yearly patterns. The snowy April in 2013 felt typical of winter instead of the spring we are accustomed to, bringing awareness of this pattern to light, although previously it was taken for granted. Climate change may bring about disruption to patterns that many of us currently don't even perceive.

People have for a long time been using these patterns for our own uses. We replicate them in our art and architecture, in our organisations and technologies, in our clothes and jewellery. From spiral staircases to roofing tiles, and website design to knitwear, they bring natural and human-made landscapes together.

Copying nature's patterns is known as biomimicry, where we ask how and why does nature do that? We also ask what doesn't nature do? When we want to create something we look to nature first and ask how does nature waterproof or strengthen using a minimal amount of material? For example, Velcro mimics the structure of burrs from the burdock plant. How hummingbirds move their wings is being studied to improve flight. This links with solutions thinking and can provide us with different insights to find a solution. We can find inspiration all around us in nature, even with our pets, such as cats showing us the warmest microclimates in the garden.

Biomimicry can be used to find solutions to move us closer to each of the three ethics. We can source inspiration from how nature repairs itself and regenerates to work on degraded landscapes and other earthcare projects. Observing other animals and how they work together and communicate can provide us with lessons of peoplecare. From nature we can learn about living in limits and balance, which is needed for fair shares.

We can look to nature for metaphors, discovering new layers of meaning through tuning in and reflecting on natural processes and other beings. For example, we can think of trees losing their leaves in autumn and how that can relate to us letting go of things. Or perhaps we can look to a favourite animal and see what lessons they have for us. We could look at cats and see how they alternate times of total relaxation with energy and focus – how can we use this metaphor of being cat-like to be at our most effective? We can take a walk through nature reflecting on our life and seeing our journey through the lens of nature.

Deep time and space

There is a continuity of evolution and co-adaptation within eco systems and within all of life. The evolution of each species is driven by needs such as food and reproduction.

We are accustomed to viewing life through human frames, understandably. The range of human experiences seems very broad until we look at the diversity of forms and behaviours in other animals, let alone when we look at plant species. Beyond the parameters of human form, movement, speed and habitats we can survive in, are extremes of temperature, size, life spans and habits. The height a flea can jump is proportionally way beyond Olympic athletes, the speed of a snail slower than our slowest walkers. There are much longer timescales inhabited by giant redwoods, and insects live in shorter timescales. While it might seem that we have inhabited the whole earth, we are yet to dwell in the sky, at the bottom of the ocean or underground as other beings do.

Animals live with different senses dominating their lives. Dogs have smell maps as well as visual maps in their minds. When we take away our human frames of experiencing the world predominately through our eyes we can open up to a world of taste, smell, touch and energy fields.

Beyond the five senses we learn about in school there is a world of senses available to us. Michael Cohen[28] identifies categories of radiation, feeling, chemical, and mental senses and lists 53 other senses in these categories we can tune in to. Radiation senses include sense of season, sense of awareness of one's own visibility or invisibility, sense of temperature and temperature change. Sense of gravity, sense of weight and balance and sense of motion are all feeling senses. There are chemical senses such as sense of appetite and hunger for food, water and air, sense of humidity including the acumen to find water or evade a flood. And mental senses consisting of sense of time, sense of fear and sense of play, pleasure and laughter amongst others. These senses are available to all of us, but some of us are naturally more connected to them, and some of us take time to develop and pay attention to them more, and for many people these different senses can be influencing our emotions, behaviour and thinking without us being consciously aware. For example, our sense of the seasons can be driving feelings of wanting to hibernate and do little, while our working lives may not support this, generating disharmony and confusion. I'm also keen on the idea of estivating, meaning to be dormant, in the summer or periods of drought, in the first hot summer for years I am definitely sensing that need.

In *Thinking like a mountain*[29] there is a workshop process called 'council of all beings'. During the council each person takes on the role of another being and talks from their viewpoint. One person may be a mountain and be able to talk from a bigger timeframe, someone else an ocean creature and communicates from the depths, another a river and speaks with the fluidity of water, another an owl contributing their stories from the sky, another a milking cow sharing her interactions with people. When we inhabit these roles we gain a deep sense of the interconnectedness of all life, feeling the effects of the actions of people on the lives of other beings. The human frame, through which we view the world, dissolves during the council and afterwards is forever softened, we can no longer return to seeing nature as a picture in the background, or something just viewed behind a television screen. Nature becomes within and without and we see ourselves as participants in nature, with a deeper sense of time and space. We see ourselves as part of a much larger ecological self, where the rainforest are our external lungs, the rivers our external veins.

Principles from nature

Permaculture has observed nature to understand the principles that make ecosystems productive, self sustaining and healthy. Using these principles in our gardens, farms, businesses, family and communities we can make them productive, self sustaining and healthy.

Nature is diverse in shape and form. We can *use and value diversity.* In our gardens growing a diverse range of plants provides resilience from pests, in our lives we can have a diversity of interests and friends to maintain healthy balance. In our groups and communities we can value diversity in people's skills, outlooks, ideas and opinions.

By responding to feedback, ecosystems can self-regulate to maintain balance. For example, predator and prey populations will pulse with each other, so that neither expands too much. *Apply self-regulation and accept feedback* reminds us to respond to the feedback we are receiving from our actions, whether this is from the reactions of our friends and family, or from observations wider afield. Many systems have become so large nowadays that the consequences are often out of sight or further downstream. Side effects are externalised, or subsidies mask the true costs. This scale means there is a lack of feedback or a deafness to the feedback we do get and hence action isn't taken and the problems get bigger.

The mega-scale, rapid expansion that we are seeing across the world in cities, corporations and farms are often beyond natural limits. Chemical fertilisers and fossil fuels permit this quick growth. The principle of *small and slow solutions* points us in the direction of organic growth and appropriate scale.

Eco-systems are able to maintain themselves with no external inputs because energy is cycled around. With *energy cycling* in mind we move away from linear processes, which require external inputs and produce waste or pollution that then need to be dealt with. Instead we try and create flows of nutrients, energy and information to meet needs. This enables us to *produce no waste*.

In a natural system all the energy comes from renewable resources. The people within our own systems are renewable resources that we can benefit from. The principle *use and value renewable resources and services* tells us that we can be confident that we have the resources we need for growth and sustenance.

Natural cycles

By being present and immersed in nature, we absorb through our pores the essence of natural life and we become aware of our own nature. When we observe wild places we can ask ourselves the question – what wild places are inside of me?

Tuning into nature we become more sensitive to our own natural flows, rhythms and cycles. Life is a cyclical process with daily, seasonal and annual cycles. We are more able to adapt to our fluctuating energy flows by seeing this pulsation as a normal part of life. Instead of fighting and trying to change these natural flows we can work with them and use their different characteristics.

This becomes a way of being, not just in our heads but permeating through our bodies. We are able to learn through our body and senses, connecting with our intuitive bodily knowing.

Opposite thinking

If we deny ourselves as part of nature and think that nature and people are separate we can experience isolation and indifference. We can be literally ungrounded. More and more people are displaying symptoms of nature deficit syndrome, such as anxiety, attention disorders and depression.[30] When we don't have nature around us and are just surrounded by screens all the time, we lose track of a natural pace of life and can become over stimulated, with images moving too rapidly for us to grasp, and hence a susceptibility to attention disorders. Losing our connection and place in the natural world can leave us feeling anxious and depressed.

Supposing that people and nature are separate is a learnt pattern of thinking from our culture with subsequent behaviours, it is not something we are born with. Michael Cohen[31] writes, "We learn to reason and live in a story and process that promotes an undeclared, hidden war against nature."

Each species on the planet has survived through adaptation. Janine Benyus[32] asks, "Are we as a species well adapted?" It can be scary to face the answers to that question; to let in observations about the taste of our food and tap water, the satisfaction and health of those around us, the energy use it takes to maintain our lifestyles. It is only by feeling the answers and letting in this knowledge can we respond appropriately.

When we don't see, value or respect the consequences of our actions for other species, a lack of responsibility arises. This lack of responsibility is true for individuals and for corporations and governments. When we place the emphasis on short-term effects for people we fail to see the longer term, wider effects for the whole planet. If we think we are different then we have the notion that we are above the laws that govern nature. There is an arrogance in placing people's needs and profits as more important. And for many of us this grates us deep down and hurts us, as we know it to be a contradiction and a falsehood to think that humanity can survive without a healthy planet. This inherent lie leads to a lack of trust. This lack of security in the future further escalates feelings of disconnection, depression and isolation.

Globally we are facing a crisis of lack of earthcare with habitat destruction, deforestation, monocultures, pollution, chemical use and the list goes on. There is a link between the lack of earthcare and the other two ethics, peoplecare and fair shares. The fair shares ethic extends to sharing the planet's resources with other beings, not just about sharing between people. And there is a mirroring of how we care for others and how we care for the Earth. These situations have arisen through ignoring feedback, overstretching natural limits, and a lack of care and connection.

Benefits of thinking like nature

When we open ourselves to nature's bounty and complexity, then mystery, awe and wonder come flooding in. When resonating with the paradox of nature's fragility and strength, feelings of responsibility and care are fostered. Respect is generated for the intelligence, beauty and wisdom of nature. When we realise that we are nature we can develop respect for our own intrinsic intelligence, wisdom and beauty; the innate intelligence that governs our breathing, heart pumping, movement and consciousness.

We can feel ourselves as part of a much bigger whole. Instead of feeling isolated within our bodies and lives, we feel a sense of kinship, community and belonging with the whole of life. Life that extends deep into the past and far into the future.

We can come to understand that there is order in the chaos of nature; with rhythms, cycles, patterns and energy flows. This can lead us to understanding our own natural rhythms, cycles, patterns and energy flows, and learning to work with the nature of these and flow more harmoniously through life. We are able to respond to life around and within us, finding a dynamic and appropriate tempo and pulsing.

Responding to life

Life is cyclical and we can tune into these cycles in our own lives. Sitting still in nature and just taking time to be allows us to take in the different paces of being. You can do this at any time, but a particularly good time is the time of transition between the seasons. As nature grows, decays, reproduces, and is dormant, you can see where this can be reflected and find metaphors for what is happening for yourself, and where your energy is wanting to flow. A classic example of this is the breaking of dormancy and the new growth that occurs in Spring, encouraging fresh starts and often initiating spring cleaning. Having what is known as a 'sit spot'[33] is helpful in observing these transitions. A sit spot is a regular place where we spend time just being still and observing.

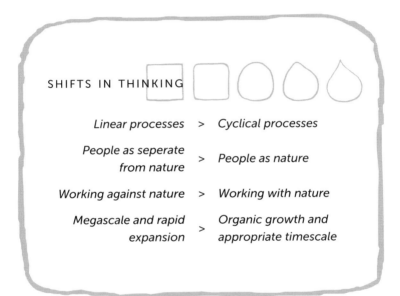

SHIFTS IN THINKING

Linear processes	>	*Cyclical processes*
People as seperate from nature	>	*People as nature*
Working against nature	>	*Working with nature*
Megascale and rapid expansion	>	*Organic growth and appropriate timescale*

CHAPTER FIVE

Co-operative Thinking

Maximum freedom to the parts,
maximum coherence to the whole.
Brian Goodwin[34]

Co-operative thinking takes us beyond thinking of ourselves. As we understand from systems thinking, we are all connected. With co-operative thinking we endeavour to create and nurture beneficial relationships. We can share identities, culture, hopes, visions and purpose with groups of people that enable us to work together effectively.

Beehive

While bees have different roles and functions within the hive they all have the same goal in mind of contributing to a healthy colony, while still maintaining freedom of individuals. Each bee makes a small contribution and together they produce a lot of honey. We can use this analogy for ourselves as part of humanity. Each of us is only one of seven billion people, but together we can work wonders. We can deliver our contributions with humility and respect for others, offering it for the greater good.

Beneficial relationships and guilds

In the garden we can create guilds of plants that can support each other with exchanges of nutrients and functions, thereby enhancing growth and productivity. A classic example of this is the guild known as the three sisters originating in South America, where the different properties of the plants are utilised. Squash, beans and sweetcorn are grown together; squash acts as ground cover helping to keep moisture in the soil, beans fix nitrogen into the soil providing nutrients for the other plants and the sweetcorn gives support for climbing beans. Together they are more fruitful and healthy than if the plants were grown separately.

With people, guilds can form in our groups and communities providing mutual support. Each person has particular characteristics and certain niches that suit them. When working together there can be exchanges of skills and ideas. A visionary and a do-er working together in a group is a potent combination when each other's attributes are acknowledged and appreciated. Relationships can be nurtured through listening, accepting different outlooks, assuming the good intentions of each other and by being warm and friendly. The closer the proximity of either plants or people to each other allows more flow and exchanges to occur. Of course there is an optimum closeness for both people and plants – too close and it can be counter productive.

The principle *integrate rather than segregate* reminds us to provide opportunities for beneficial relationships to occur by bringing things together. When people are brought together, unexpected things can and do happen. From systems thinking we know that synergy and emergence will occur. This is the place of hope, possibility and magic. We are not just blindly optimistic for the future because it is realistic to expect the unexpected. We can be *possibilitists* – aware of the infinite possibilities that await us.

Power-with rather than power-over

Power is defined by the dictionary as 'the control and influence *over* other people and their actions.' This traditional view of power can be thought of as *power-over* characterised by domination and hierarchy. With power-over there is only one or maybe a few leaders, and the rest of us are there to be controlled. Communication and feedback often only flow in one direction – from the top. This type of power stifles our creativity and resourcefulness.

Another dictionary definition of power is 'the ability, skill or capacity to do something.' Using this definition we can come to recognise a different kind of power – *power-with*. This is where our ability to do something increases when we work together. In power-with situations there are many channels of communication and influence between all the members. Power-with can be viewed as a state of being and receptiveness. We are able to honour each other's personalities, skills, life experiences and talents.

We are also able to accommodate differences of opinions. The principle of *use edge and value the marginal* is helpful, to allow us to embrace times when there are differences and to assist us in finding a meeting place of ideas and views. The edge is the most fertile place and can bring about solutions that we would not have arrived at independently.

Starling murmurations work because the interest of the individual is the same as the interest of the collective. Together there is safety in numbers from predator birds.

The idea of co-operative thinking and power-with could be extended into classrooms and instead of each individual needing to get good grades to move up, it would be fun to imagine the differences if the whole class needed to pass to move on. The more able students would need to focus their attention on helping the other students. Each student would develop a social responsibility encouraging them to try their hardest. There is a parallel here with challenges that humanity face at the moment. We all need to face these crises together and move forward together. We need to find solutions that work for all, not just for some.

This century we could be moving into wars for water. Instead of competing for water and paying little consequence to what happens outside of our borders, we could move to co-operating and finding the best ways to use it for everyone's benefit. We could recognise that ultimately we are all downstream of our own pollution. We need to acknowledge that together we are the 100%; we are all in the same boat and we need to operate from a position of power-with to ensure that our boat doesn't sink.

Co-creating

When thinking co-operatively we are aware of our actions contributing to the greater whole, just like in the beehive, even though our actions can seem small in themselves. Each action has ripples that are beyond what we are able to trace. In *Blessed Unrest* Paul Hawken talks about this unnamed movement that is happening globally, where hundreds of thousands, possibly millions of organisations are working towards a better world. Whether their focus is on environmental protection, social justice or personal development and healing, they all have in mind a commitment to make things better. Each one of these organisations can seem such a small dot but when viewed together they can be seen as the pixels on a photo and a larger image becomes clear. Each of our gardens can be seen as separate, with defining borders, but wildlife see the corridors and connections between them. Similarly there are threads of connections and themes that run through these disparate organisations. Paul Hawken calls this the largest social movement in history that is restoring grace, justice and beauty to the world.

When asked if I am pessimistic or optimistic about the future my answer is always the same: if you look at science that describes what is happening on Earth today and aren't pessimistic, you don't have the right data. If you meet the people in this unnamed movement and aren't optimistic, you haven't got a heart.

Paul Hawken[35]

This optimism can take nourishment from the concept of emergence, knowing that as we all come together, something stronger can arise. Collaboration can bring forth playful discovery.

I am part of *Thriving Ways*, a new collective of people and permaculture facilitators, who have come together to support and collaboratively develop and market our courses and resources. We realised that if we act together we are able to develop more of a presence to promote our courses and create right livelihoods for ourselves, as well as supporting each other.

It is through coming together and sharing our diverse skills and experiences that we find better solutions. There can be unity and strength in our co-creating through valuing our diversity. Some people work best at the front, others are good at fulfilling supportive roles, suggestive of mycelium working underground. Teamwork is at its best when we are inspired to be our full selves and value each others' contributions.

The incongruity of anarchists, billionaire funders, street clowns, scientists, youthful activists, indigenous and native people, diplomats, computer geeks, writers, strategists, peasants and students all working toward common goals is a testament to human impulses that are unstoppable and eternal.

Paul Hawken[36]

Collective circle of influence

Steven Covey[37] describes a circle of influence that each of us has. Surrounding this is a circle of concern, containing issues we want to change but aren't currently able to influence. For most of us we have many things in our circles of concern – everything from the future of our children to climate change, from melting ice caps to security of our jobs, from starving children in far away lands to the homeless on the streets in our town. We can start to feel quite overwhelmed in the face of these challenges, and become stuck in feelings of 'I can't' and not knowing where or how to start to change things.

It is useful to not perceive our circle of influence as fixed but something that fluctuates over time and there can be solutions that come into sight that were previously unattainable. When we expand our circle of influence we can bring about changes to issues in our circles of concern.

When we open ourselves up to thinking co-operatively we can find refuge in a collective circle of influence that is substantially more expansive than our individual circles of influence. We could use patterns of nature to find ways to increase our collective circle of influence. The success of flocking or herding pattern is from large numbers coming together. Together we can make more noise, such as with online petitions. Another way is to create a chain of people that are able to influence a concern. One person leads to another, for example a friend's mother's uncle's boss knows someone who can talk to a politician, school governor, CEO etc. The spiral pattern shows how influence can grow incrementally, slowly working its way outwards.

Overlapping our circle of influence is a circle of care, and through acknowledging and embracing that we can expand our feelings of interconnectedness. One day perhaps our circles of care will not have anyone or anything outside of it.

From systems thinking we know that all systems are connected, so when there is a core of people working together they have influence within each of the systems they are part of, and hence the collective circle of influence of any group of people is much wider and greater than the sum of its parts.

We move from 'I can't' to 'we can'. *We can* come together to build our collective potential, to collaborate and create solutions. *We can* face our concerns and make a difference.

Opposite thinking

When we are thinking in terms of competition instead of co-operation we can fall into the scarcity mindset where there can only be one winner. It can be argued that competition has led us to develop our skills further and push ahead. In some cases this happens, it is also true that competition can also have the opposite effect. When competition is involved some people stop trying if they believe they will never be that sole winner. In workplaces where competition is dominant it is difficult for people to move forward when they are metaphorically watching their backs.

When racing to the finish line it is easy to be neglectful of the consequences you leave behind. In business this can often be seen where it is more important to be the cheapest, smartest and best and the costs for the environment or workers are not taken into account.

When thinking in terms of competition we lose opportunities to collaborate with others and create better solutions than we could by ourselves.

There is an undermining belief in our society that relationships are hard, full of challenges and will probably fall apart. This belief has gained ground in the last few decades with the rise of divorces.

Instead of a co-operative mindset we would be thinking individualistically. This can leave us feeling isolated and lonely. In cities and towns, instead of welcoming and benefiting from an abundance of people, a collective separation is experienced when we view ourselves as individuals. When we place ourselves on an island it is harder to perceive other factors acting upon our lives. Both our illnesses and our health are seen as individual and not part of a larger system. For example, many health problems arise from systems of food production and cultural eating habits, rather than inherent defects in our bodies. Another example is the natural responses that can occur when we witness the state of the world. All too often though, it is viewed as unnatural to become depressed or cry or be angry; we are supposed to be numb to others and just be focused on how life is for us.

Robert Holden[38] identifies a dysfunctional independence, where we try and do too much by ourselves. It is dysfunctional because we do not live in isolation, every meal we eat is proof that we are dependant on other people, other species and sun, rain and soil. We forget all the help and support that could be available to us. He says, "Asking for help is a good thing, a wise thing, it's not illegal, it's not a failure, it's not wrong." And yet the focus and learnt behaviours of individualism have led us to view ourselves as separate beings that must stand alone, and asking for help or engaging support is frowned upon. By not asking for help, the opportunity for someone to give help and feel connected and valued is also lost. Furthermore, this individualistic viewpoint can lead us to taking all the credit for our own successes and not acknowledging the support and influences from others.

Benefits of co-operative thinking

Thich Nhat Hanh[39] describes in his poem '*interbeing*' how everything is connected with a piece of paper: the sun, clouds, loggers, and the wheat that provides the loggers' daily bread, everything comes together to create this one piece of paper.

> *Everything co-exists in the sheet of paper. 'To be' is 'to inter-be'. You cannot just be by yourself, alone. You have to inter-be with every other thing. This sheet of paper is because everything else is.*
>
> Thich Nhat Hanh

When we fully embrace the idea of inter-being we want to work with others more explicitly, we want to create more connections and work through a model of power-with, because it makes sense.

When we recognise that we are all working for a joint purpose we can move from blame to compassion, and understanding that we are all doing the best we can, given our circumstances.

With co-operative thinking we shift our thinking from 'power-over', where one person is right and there is one right way of doing things. We open up to different ways of thinking and being that can complement each other. Instead of one person being in charge with all the answers we find strength in acting together, we come to a place of 'power-with'. We can think like a global family.

Discovering abundance

Through asking and offering help to the people around us we are able to build social capital and deepen our connections. Through synergy and emergence there is abundance to be found. You can shift into a mindset of co-creation, and engage others by recognising the times you need help or resources and actually being specific in requesting them, as well as being available to help others.

SHIFTS IN THINKING

I can't	>	*We can*
Blame	>	*Compassion*
Power-over	>	*Power-with*
One right way	>	*Diversity of ways*
Have to do it all myself	>	*Co-creation*
Dysfunctional independence	>	*Recognising and valuing our 'inter-being'*

CHAPTER SIX

Thinking for the Future

What we imagine in our minds becomes our world.
Dr Emoto[40]

There are many futures we could focus on, the futures within our lifetimes, and those beyond. When we open up to considering beyond the present day and short-term gains, we open up to our responsibilities, new possibilities, responding to change and accepting and accounting for consequences. We are the ancestors of the future – what will they be thankful to us for?

Parent and child

As children grow and develop, they need nurturing and guidance. As they grow, their needs change and parents have to be responsive to those changes. Parents need to allow their child's future to unfold and follow its own course, *and* parents can provide the right conditions for growth.

Children can be seen to hold the potential of all people. The child can be a symbol for the potential of our time in history. Children are symbolic of our need to take responsibility for the direction of our future.

Planning ahead

Whatever we do today has effects in the future. We can be kind to our future selves even with small acts such as preparing for our day tomorrow, filing our paperwork and cooking dinner in advance. When we plant seeds, literal or otherwise we are thinking of our future selves that might one day benefit from the harvest.

When we put money into savings we are making investments in the future. Judicious use of resources allow us to save and conserve for the future. This is one of the major flaws in the industrial culture – we are consuming more and more of the world's resources without replenishing them and without thinking about how future generations will survive.

In abundance thinking we used the principle *catch and store energy* to remind us to capture seasonal flows. We can have stores of produce, firewood, water and seeds. We can move from being a consumer to someone who creates and produces. With the principle *obtain a yield* we are focused on gaining from our work. While we need short-term gains to feed us, maintain interest and give us motivation and momentum, it is also crucial that we design for long-term productivity as well. Our actions of today are an investment in our future.

Developing the vision

Part of planning ahead is deciding where we want to end up. As with any journey it is more probable we will reach our destination if we set out with that intention and plan our way there. We also need awareness of where we are starting from by observing our current state (which in itself is affected by our past). We can then plan steps to move us from where we are to where we want to be. The more texture and detail we have for our vision the more achievable and real it will seem, making a positive outcome more probable.

When we pay attention to our vision we are making an active decision about the future we are choosing for ourselves. Small changes in the present can lead to a big difference in destination in the future. Just simply the act of shifting our trajectory will land us in a different place. The same is true for the direction of humanity. A slight shift in our perspective and taking responsibility for the direction we move in, can take us to a completely different place. We can be responsive to new circumstances and keep monitoring our progress to check it is in the direction we are wanting.

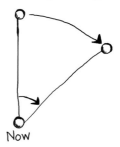

Now

Succession in nature

In ecosystems there is a natural process of change and development known as succession. As conditions change, different species find their niches. In the early stages pioneers come in, they themselves create the fertility and other conditions suitable for secondary species. Later these will give way to climax species.

We can observe and account for succession in our own systems. In groups, for example we can be aware that people have different preferences and skills suitable for varying stages in a group's life, such as pioneers who thrive on creating something new and people who prefer to maintain growth and development over time.

Future of humanity

When we think about the future of humanity and the planet there is a big question about whether things are getting better or worse. The answer depends upon where you look, how you ask, who you ask, what you measure, how you measure and so on. Statistics can be manipulated to show what is wanted.

As Paul Hawken said, he is pessimistic looking at the science and optimistic when looking at all the people working for change. It is not just as simple as whether we are being optimistic or pessimistic – there is also being realistic and 'possible-istic'. The realistic thing is that the future is uncertain and unpredictable and new possibilities and opportunities will surely arise. It is not in the mainstream paradigm for us to be excited about the future, either for ourselves or for humanity. The messages are that uncertainty isn't favourable and we should insure ourselves against it. We are taught to protect ourselves against this unpredictability.

It would be radical to suggest that we can be excited about what's around the corner. We could be excited about possibilities for technological breakthroughs, greater community cohesion, nutritious food for all, secure livelihoods and enhanced well-being. All of these things are believable in the future of humanity. When we open up to thinking in terms of abundance and solutions then these things seem not only possible, but more probable. This is the story of *the Great Turning* that we can inhabit.

Alongside this though, we have to embrace the uncertainty that we don't know how things will turn out, we don't know if we will escape *the Great Unravelling*. But rather than this uncertainty directing us towards hopelessness and inaction, we can choose to give it the best of our abilities. We can dedicate all our courage, ingenuity and co-operation to service of life on Earth.

There are elements of what we, as humanity, are doing now that could be present in both the best and worst possible scenarios for the future. Similarly we can observe what is happening around us now that is a result of actions from the past, we can accept feedback of those past actions and respond differently now. Unfortunately there is often a resistance to change, as individuals and cultures we can cling to habits of the past. Even when we are suffering ill effects from actions of the past, we can still be attached to those very same actions, such as a smoker with lung cancer.

However, change is inevitable no matter how much we might try and resist or control it. Whether it is climate change or social change, the world will be different in 100 years time. It is not just peak oil that we are facing but peak copper, uranium, phosphate etc. The question now facing humanity is not whether things will change, but how and when. There are times in our lives where sinuous pathways carve out new directions and other times when there are sharp hairpin bends and turning points. The same is true collectively as for individually – are we going to see abrupt or gradual changes? When we see change as necessary we are more able to make our own adaptations and direct the process of change, rather than being blown around by it.

We need to recover our respect for water and all of life, deciding what we want our future to look like, such as forecasting there to be plentiful, pure water for all.

The saying 'the best time to plant a tree is 20 years ago – the second best time is now' informs us that it is never too late to influence the future. It is only by losing hope and not doing anything that we lose our chance to have a positive impact in the future. For ourselves, George Eliott reminds us, "It is never too late to be what you might have been." And the Earth has a chance to be what might have been with more ecological thinking and care.

Deep time

We move into deep time again, where time is elastic and stretches in circles around us. The past and the future flow through the present in a continuous stream. There are no solid boundaries between past, present and future.

Over seven years every cell of our body is reformed. The cells of our skin fall into dust in the air landing on soil to be digested by worms and then plants take up nutrients from worm casts, in turn plants are eaten and digested, and so on with molecules assembling and disassembling over time, from being to being. In this way our physical structure is as old as the Earth itself.

Life is a continuous journey; there is an unbroken line of humanity. When we were no more than a mere egg of potentiality we were inside our mother's womb when she was a baby growing inside her mother. The egg that will be my grandchild lived inside my daughter's womb while she was housed in my womb.

If we were to view the entire four and a half billion years of history of the Earth and it's inhabitants over a 24-hour period, humans would only be around in the last five seconds. Can we imagine the next 24-hour period of the future of the Earth? While people in the past have taken the continuity of life for granted it is now not a foregone conclusion that life will continue to be sustained by the planetary system we are putting under stress. This severe threat to our very existence provides a backdrop of insecurity. We need to learn to live with this insecurity and use it as a motivator rather than allowing it to hinder us.

Opening up to these larger timescales provides us with a bigger picture that includes both greater possibilities and responsibilities. Thinking in much larger timescales can be both overwhelming and a reassuring relief.

Native Americans contemplate the seventh generation

– 200 years in the future, when our great grandchildren will have great grandchildren. Our ancestors would plant oak trees ready to replace the oak beams used in building, knowing that it would be the seventh generation that would have this job to do, when the oak trees would be the right size. Opening up to deep time involves expanding the time for both the negative consequences of our actions and the fruits of our labours. We move from quick fixes to longer lasting results from starting with *small and slow solutions.*

Imagine being at a storyteller's convention 500 years in the future, where storytellers tell tales of this time in history known as *the Great Turning*, where people took courageous actions to protect the Earth and create alternative ways of living. With the benefit of hindsight and a larger time perspective we would be able to see the entire arc of change that we are currently part of. The individual stories would have a very different complexion when seen as part of a bigger story.

Living in the present

Currently the speed we are living is increasing, we are living life faster and faster in the modern world, resembling a drumbeat speeding up until it can't be sustained any longer. As we are more and more dependent on computer time and instant emails and messaging, we lose a sense of thoughtfulness and relaxation with time to spend. As we struggle and hurry to keep up with the demands on the present we lose contact with the past and future.

While thinking for the future is important it is also worth us remembering to live in the present, to savour the present moment without rushing ahead. We don't want to be so caught up with the future that we forget to enjoy life as it is now. Part of thinking abundantly is to appreciate what is, rather than hankering after what could be.

Opposite thinking

Being unconcerned for the future has led to absurd situations such as built in obsolescence where the most important thing is current profit. Waste, pollution and lack of resources in the future do not come into the picture. We are currently living in a world where short-term gain outweighs long-term security. The consequences of our actions are placed out of sight, where we are blind to thinking for the future.

We can become preoccupied with a narrow 'now', consumed by the trivia of our lives, unable to expand our views.

The quick fix and rapid growth mindset leaves us reactive to problems as they arise, rather than anticipating what might happen and trying to be preventative.

Governments make decisions based on electoral timeframes, and with a new government in place every few years, mistakes are constantly being remade. There is a lack of continuity in thinking and preparedness.

Benefits of thinking for the future

On a personal level thinking for the future makes us more resilient and helps provide security. On individual and collective levels planning ahead can save us a lot of time, energy and money in the long run, through us having longer lasting solutions and not having to repair previous mistakes. When we are able to visualise future generations our lives and actions have more meaning.

When we think for the future we can embrace potential and imagine what is possible. Then we can move beyond that to really dream the world we want to create, the world more wonderful than even our imagination dares to go.

Embracing potential

Each new day is an opportunity to excel, develop, dream, enact, expand, grow and flourish. Think about tomorrow and the week ahead. What can you do for yourself today that lays strong foundations for you to be at your finest in the future? This may be tidying your work space, ensuring you get enough sleep, laying a fire in advance or imagining success. Imagine yourself to be your own best friend, providing little actions of practical support. Seeing the potential to thrive in each new day leads us into action.

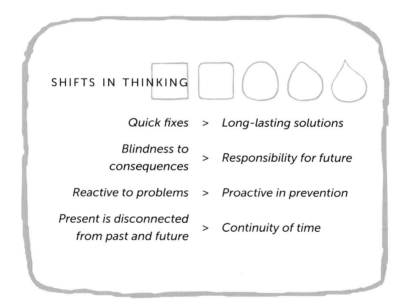

SHIFTS IN THINKING

Quick fixes	>	Long-lasting solutions
Blindness to consequences	>	Responsibility for future
Reactive to problems	>	Proactive in prevention
Present is disconnected from past and future	>	Continuity of time

CHAPTER SEVEN

From Thinking to Doing

Only through action can you bring a vision to life.
Deepak Chopra[41]

Moving to doing is essential on our personal and collective journeys to improving our lives. All the thinking in the world won't resolve the problems – action is crucial. Our actions can inspire others and demonstrate to the world what is possible.

Each way of thinking can become manifest in our actions, and there is also the benefit of focusing on this shift to action as a specific way of being focused on bringing changes into our lives.

With moving from thinking into doing, we drop into our bodies. There is an integration process between body and mind, thoughts and action, internal and external. It is through integration that we bring about positive change in our lives and the world.

Frog jumping

The frog jumping is our symbol for the movement from thinking to doing. The frog is actively choosing movement, and here we make active choices about how our new thinking can manifest in the world. When a frog jumps momentum is needed for take-off. There is always somewhere for it to land when it jumps; when we move forward we can trust there is somewhere for our path to take us. As a friend summarised, sometimes change is more than a step by step process, there are times when it is step, step, leap, change.

Being and doing

There is a balance between who we are in the world and what we do – our being and our doing. Ideally our being and doing complement and enhance each other and there is a congruency between them. With shifting our thinking and opening up to new possibilities we will want to step forward into an invigorating future. Moving forward can involve both going forth and going in, expanding our doing and being. Going in involves building our inner resources in whatever ways are appropriate for us. Our being is about how we feel about the world and ourselves; our being relates to our responses and urges for our doing. If we imagine a lake, there is plenty of activity below the surface and ripples can come from below. Insects, wind and other activity on the surface also create ripples.

Within each of us are seeds waiting to grow, which can germinate given suitable conditions. Sometimes our initial focus needs to be on creating the right circumstances for those seeds to break open and sprout shoots. Sometimes we need to focus our attention internally, to create the foundations of strength and resourcefulness before we can move forward with direction and vigour.

Thinking differently awakens unfamiliar aspects of ourselves. Different qualities are brought forth through our thinking – our courage, creativity, resilience, satisfaction, awe, passion and ingenuity can all be stirred into play. With these awake in us we can move forward with purpose and energy.

Shifting our thinking will alter our behaviours. However, this isn't always immediate, there can be a time lag between shifting our internal thinking and changing our external behaviours. The delay between our thinking and our behaviours changing can be anything from five seconds to five years. Sometimes we can find ourselves doing something while internally we know there is a dissonance with our thoughts; how we want to behave and how we are actually behaving. This can be disheartening, and we may wonder if we were almost better off when we were blind to this. This stage of becoming aware is necessary though and we can celebrate our awareness knowing that it can lead us forward.

Process versus static thinking

In systems thinking we learnt to be aware of flow as opposed to stuff. This is also a shift from static to process[42] or sequential thinking.

With static thinking we are confined by what is in our frame and we see what is in front of us as fixed, like a photograph that cannot change. We see the reality of the world as rigid. The view we have of ourselves is also predetermined. However, life is more like a film in action rather than a photo. In process thinking we become aware of our actions being part of a sequence. When we move into action each step takes us forward into the next frame.

With animations the next image is just slightly different from the previous frame, each one slowly adapting and evolving. Sometimes though, transformations can be a sudden change of scene, and brings to mind the concept of discontinuous change. Instead of gradual, steady and incremental growth, there can be dramatic leaps, or a sudden transformation. For example, when whipping cream, it can feel like nothing is happening for ages, and then suddenly it's whipped. Learning to ride a bike is another example where it can feel like there is no improvement and all of a sudden your body understands the balancing that it needs to do and off you go.

As Martha Lasley[43] describes, "Transformation arrives spontaneously in unlikely moments." With this in mind we can trust that our actions, no matter how small, are all contributing to a bigger picture of positive change and growth in the world and in our lives. They are all part of a bigger flow, even though this flow can be outside of our frame of awareness. This book is part of a flow of wisdom and motivation for change that has come from many sources. This flow will continue into your life, combining with your existing knowledge and becoming a part of the flow, wherever you take it in the future. These flows converge and mingle, diverge and meander.

Our long-term goals and visions

We can take time to envision our goals, and open up our long-term visions. We can do this in a method known as 'un-boundaried dreaming'; where we take away the voice that censors our visions and screens them for what we believe to be possible. We can describe what we would love to happen without the voice saying 'that would never happen/I can't do that/only millionaires or famous people could make that happen...' If we can answer what we would love to happen *as if*; *as if* I know I will be successful, *as if* I have all the resources of the universe available to me, *as if* anything is possible.

When we articulate these dreams we are then able to recognise when opportunities cross our paths that could become steps on our journey to those goals.

We all have comfort zones of who we are and what we are currently able to do. Around this is our stretch zone, where we are able to do things with more conscious effort. This stretch zone can be seen as our growing edge, the edge between our present and future selves. Beyond the stretch zone is unfamiliar territory. Our goals and visions are currently in that unknown zone. We can move into our stretch zone to gain sight of them, taking small steps to help us grow in the direction of our goals.

We can grow our edges of being and doing. For example, I am starting a permaculture training and demonstration centre with my family. Amongst other things, I have identified that I need to develop my practical skills – part of my doing. As this project will involve many people, I also recognise the need to expand my comfort zones around working with others, and finding more ways to co-create and collaborate – developing my edges of being.

Furthermore, as we develop our growing edges, our goals and visions can expand and develop and we are able to see more texture and detail to them.

When we are clear on our vision, we can maximise our actions in this direction. We can have maximum intention and minimum effort. All of our efforts are channelled into this goal and we don't get distracted or waste time and energy. The focus and clarity allows us to venture forward purposefully.

Action learning cycle

There are four stages to the action learning cycle. We move from designing to doing to reflecting to thinking and researching to designing and round again.

We can start at any stage. One of the principles to help us begin is to *design from patterns to details.* Outlined in the previous chapters are patterns of thinking, now you can think of the details of your situation. You can move from these overall patterns into specifics of your circumstances, passions and skills.

The most effective learning comes when we have a balance of all of these stages. With each stage there are pitfalls if we either spend too long in one stage or miss stages or spend too little time. Too much designing and designs can just end up never moving from paper into reality. Too little designing and we lose the chance to make mistakes on paper instead of the real thing. If we spend too much time doing, without reflecting on our actions, we lose the chance to re-evaluate the direction we are taking.

When we spend time reflecting, we are able to observe the effects of our actions. Which leads us into researching alternatives, and how to improve things and what our next steps will be. Observing the effects of our actions allows us to tweak what we are doing and prevents us from repeating the same mistakes over and over. We might also find that things are working better than expected and we can expand our horizons.

When my partner and myself were starting to search for some land to buy for our education centre, we carried out a design process. The design focused on how we were going to find land, rather than what we were going to do with it when we found it. We reflected upon previous attempts and then focused on unifying our ideas as well as generating possibilities. Through this design process we gained clarity, conviction and confidence. We acted together with purpose and were able to share our vision with others. Our design has been a wonderful success story, with us finding a stunning piece of land, and we are now embarking on the next design of creating the centre.

Balancing our doing

Too much doing and we can wear ourselves out. For each of us and within our families and relationships, we have different warning signals when we are doing too much. Illnesses, arguments, tears, over or under eating or sleeping can appear as signs that we are doing too much. It is important to know when to sit back and relax, reflect, dream and plan. There are different times of the day, week, month or year that suit either action or reflection more. When we can work or flow with these different energies we find it easier to achieve a balance. The principle of *applying self-regulation* can assist in us finding a workable balance.

Part of abundance thinking is to accommodate feelings of enough, we can turn this focus to ourselves and be content with what we are able to achieve and not constantly wanting ourselves to do more. Alongside this we can find ourselves in a flow of abundance, whether it is with job opportunities, an abundant garden or a life full of friendships, with these new abundances we might find ourselves initially over-whelmed. Rather than trying to stop the flow, we need to find ways in which we can work with the flow. We perhaps need ways to be more organised and more effective. We can grow into alignment with our abundances.

Small achievable steps

Every journey starts with a single step, no matter how small, it is the beginning. Starting with small practical steps that we know are achievable can help us to build a pattern of success and encourage us to go further. Micro-movements with tiny baby steps that take us less than 10 minutes can still help us start our journey.

As we build momentum there can be a succession of actions, we can start with simple, easy ones and move onto those that are less straightforward, with our actions growing in complexity as our capacity increases. Our actions can stretch us and we can be responsive to the expanding possibilities available as we do more, feeling our way forward with each step.

A useful place to start is the place where our efforts will have the most effect. The principle *minimum effort for maximum effect* directs us to actions that are least effort and will have most impact. If you imagine a really messy room, you can have more of an impact by tidying away the big things from the floor first. This change can then give you the motivation to go on to tidy away other areas. This is contrasted with sorting out one drawer of little things, after the same amount of time the former will have more visible effects. A useful starting point is to block energy leaks; anything that is dissipating your mental or physical energy. Doing the actions that have the most impact allows you to receive short-term benefits that can inspire further action.

Resources and limits

Whenever we embark on any project or adventure we need resources for our journey. Mapping these out can help us to feel supported. We have both inner resources and outer resources that we can draw upon.

We will also face limits or blocks upon our journey, identifying them can help us to put strategies in place for when we do encounter them. We might also realise that there are obstacles we place on the path ourselves. For example, perhaps we fill our time so we don't have enough time for our priorities.

Water has several strategies for overcoming obstacles; water can wait until there is enough volume to burst over, it can crash through, flow around or under, dissolve them over time.

Three steps to our own participation

Bill Mollison, co-founder of permaculture, describes three steps each of us can take in our everyday lives that help us to participate in the healing of our world.

Align ourselves with like-minded people

Reduce our own consumption of non-renewable resources

Connect with the growing cycle

Each of these can in turn support and be supported by the seven ways of thinking, as well as bringing the ethics to life. These steps help build our resources as well as over-coming limits.

When we align ourselves with like-minded people, our influence and effectiveness can grow. Linking arms with others, we are strengthened and synergies are created, as observed in systems thinking. This also connects with co-operative thinking and how beneficial relationships can reinforce our ideas and create more impact. Some projects are only possible through working together. The peoplecare ethic is supported with us meeting our needs of friendship, belonging and support.

Reducing our own consumption of non-renewable resources is a responsible act that demonstrates our thinking for the future. When we think in terms of abundance and balance we can reduce our dependencies and open more to the flow. With solutions thinking, we are more able to find solutions and ways of meeting our needs with the resources we have around us, rather than relying on our purchasing ability to do this. By doing this, we are moving towards living within limits and sharing more equally the available resources, in line with the fair shares ethic.

When we connect with the growing cycle, whether it is through directly growing food ourselves, or buying seasonally from a farmer's market, we become more in tune with nature's rhythms. We can connect with nature's growth through observation, observing what is in flower, and how they come into flowering earlier or later in different areas. These observations help us to think like nature and tune into our own natural rhythms and cycles. This brings the earthcare ethic to life for us in our own lives.

With these three steps we are supporting our move from thinking to doing.

Showing up

The most important thing to create change is to show up. With any creative project whether it is drawing, weaving, sculpture or writing we need to show up and be present to make it happen. When we just ponder it in our heads and dream about finding the time to do it, this is where it stays – in our heads. When we make time and sit with intent to create then something happens. When we put pen to paper or sit with paintbrush in hand we open up to something emerging. In *Juicy pens, thirsty paper* SARK[44] gives great advice for anyone wanting to write; she says, the tools we need to write are pen and paper or a computer, but in order to actually be writing we need to *move the tools.* We can come back and polish up on the quality later, but to begin just showing up and moving the tools is sufficient. The sentences that emerge from me sitting down today are different to what I might have written yesterday or tomorrow. We can't be sure what is around the corner, or what opportunities we will miss if we postpone our actions.

With life and the adventure and challenges we are currently facing we can make the commitment to show up, to be present to the story of *the Great Turning*. And, as is the same with any creative project, we don't know where it will take us and what the outcome will be, but we can be sure that something will happen when we allow it to. Whether it is about showing up and developing our skills, signing petitions, nurturing our relationships, joining a community project, or sharing our wisdom, we are investing our energies in having a positive impact on the Earth. We can commit to contributing our gifts to the service of all life on Earth, without knowing the details of where that path will take us.

Opposite thinking

If we do not move into action, we can feel overwhelmed and helpless. We can get caught in thinking that we are unable to make a difference. If we do not progress forward with our actions then our thinking also becomes static. Without action, there are no feedback loops to help us update and expand our thinking.

There is a definition of insanity – doing the same thing and expecting different results. We can be busy with actions but not thinking about them or their consequences. We can continue to make the same mistakes. Changes in our actions arise out of shifts in our thinking, rather than just acting on automatic pilot. We can allow our shifts in thinking to direct our actions. Without thinking first, we can be busy with doing but not necessarily in the direction we want.

Benefits of moving from thinking to doing

We can gain deep satisfaction from knowing that we are contributing to the solutions for the world. It is reassuring to take responsibility for our own futures. As they say actions speak louder than words, and it is our actions that first become visible to others. Through our actions we can inspire, educate and motivate others. The key point is to enjoy the path you are on, find joy in the journey and celebrate achievements.

Embracing, responding and discovering

In moving from thinking to action, embracing, responding and discovering come together.

Imagine yourself in one year's time – you may have a particular project in mind or just thinking generally about your life – embrace the potential of who you can become and all the benefits you will gain. Imagine the flow and the bigger picture of change in the world you are contributing to. Now think about potential limits you may meet on the way. Visualise yourself responding to these and overcoming them. Any patterns of procrastination can be replaced with patterns of effectiveness. Imagine yourself as water flowing around any obstacles that may appear. You are flexible and fluid, able to think and respond in the moment, never getting stuck.

The bigger picture of your long terms goals and visions is made up of smaller steps along the way. List some rewards for yourself along your path. Instead of just focusing on the end point, be grateful for the journey, and focus on the gifts and benefits you will experience on the way. Through this you will discover abundance and joy on the path.

SHIFTS IN THINKING

Consumer	>	*Producer*
Disengagement	>	*Responsibility*
Disempowerment	>	*Empowerment*
Random activity	>	*Being and doing in the direction of our visions and goals*
We are too small to make a difference	>	*Our actions have ripples*

Closing Words

It may be provocative to propose that what humanity needs at the moment is a change of thinking while problems pile up around us. However, if we do not change the thinking that created these problems they are probably going to reoccur and it is akin to mopping up the floor without turning off the overflowing tap.

Donella Meadows asserts that changing paradigms – the mind-set out of which the system – its goals, structure, rules, delays, parameters arise – is one of the most effective ways of changing a system. "You could say that paradigms are harder to change than anything else about a system… but there's nothing physical or expensive or even slow in the process of paradigm change. In a single individual it can happen in a millisecond. All it takes is a click in the mind, a falling of scales from the eyes, a new way of seeing. Whole societies are another matter – they resist challenges to their paradigms harder than they resist anything else. So how do you change paradigms?... You keep pointing at the anomalies and failures in the old paradigm. You keep speaking and acting, loudly and with assurance, from the new one."[45]

These different ways of thinking overlap, reinforce and enhance each other. When used together they create new synergies and emergence, making their use more potent. I have experienced and observed them making a huge difference, to my own and others' well-being, motivation and aspirations.

When you try them yourself be receptive to the feedback of any changes. Harvest and celebrate the gifts from your journey. Seeing with new eyes is a continual process, as we do so our seeing changes. Each day fresh things unfold, and new situations arise that allow us to put it into practice. It may be subtle changes at first, simple awareness of new words in your vocabulary that hint to the shifts that are occurring.

There will be times when it all seems very simple and obvious. And other times when cultural conditioning, social groups and media don't support these different ways of thinking and it can feel as though you are swimming upstream. These are times to reach out and find support. From here, there are many places you can go to develop and embed your thinking. *People &Permaculture* has many activities to take this thinking further into different aspects of our lives and society. There are plenty of courses, workshops, books, films and websites, for permaculture, the Work That Reconnects and many other approaches to further your thinking and action.

At this pivotal time in human history we all have choices to make. Do we choose to believe in positive change? Do we choose to use our courage and skills and to fully enter into the flow of life? Do we choose to step up and make a difference – to do the things we may have been wishing someone else would do? We can choose to be the ones we have been waiting for.

This is an invitation to embark on a beautiful journey of embracing, responding and discovering.

What you really know is possible in your heart is possible.

Dr Emoto[46]

Ways of Thinking Summary

Way of Thinking	Example	Permaculture Principle
Abundance Thinking	Observing with an attitude of gratitude and abundance enables us to connect more with our real wealth.	Observe and interact
	Catching energy when there are flows to store for when there are ebbs in energy.	Catch and store energy
	Gaining benefits from our activities.	Obtain a yield
	Reframing waste as resources and finding uses for them.	Produce no waste
Solutions Thinking	Working steadily can bring us lasting change, instead of quick fixes we have longer lasting results.	Small and slow solutions
	Identifying the defining characteristics of a problem and find ways in which we can utilise these features.	The problem is the solution
	The changing context of problems can reveal solutions that were previously unavailable.	Creatively use and respond to change
	Research and creativity can lead to enhancing and improving what we are doing.	Yield is limited only by the imagination and information of the designer
Systems Thinking	Bringing things together encourages exchanges and creates conditions for synergy and emergence.	Integrate rather than segregate
Thinking Like Nature	Valuing the diversity of skills, outlooks, ideas and opinions in our groups and communities.	Use and value diversity

Way of Thinking	Example	Permaculture Principle
Thinking Like Nature	Responding to informal and formal feedback that we receive from family and friends and use this to adapt our actions and self-regulate.	Apply self-regulation and accept feedback
	Growing organically at an appropriate scale.	Use small and slow solutions
	Creating flows of nutrients, energy and information to meet needs.	Energy cycling
	Using renewable resources of people to meet needs of entertainment, play, comfort etc.	Use and value renewable resources and services
Co-operative Thinking	Bringing people together allows for unexpected things to occur.	Integrate rather than segregate
	Embracing the differences between people and finding meeting places of ideas and viewpoints.	Use edge and value the marginal
Thinking for the Future	Storing firewood, seeds, water for the future.	Catch and store energy
	Planning for the future, we are reminded to have short-term gains that provide momentum and help us maintain interest.	Obtain a yield
From Thinking to Doing	Self-regulating to find a balance between our being and doing in the world.	Apply self-regulation and accept feedback
	Moving from overall patterns of thinking to the specifics for our own lives.	Designing from patterns to details
	Finding actions that will have the most impact in our lives for the least change.	Minimum effort and maximum effect

Resources

Books

Active Hope – How to Face the Mess We're in Without Going Crazy; Joanna Macy, Chris Johnstone; New World Library, 2012.

Be The Change – Action and Reflection from People Transforming Our World; Interviews by Trenna Cormack; Love Books, 2007.

Beyond You and Me – Inspirations and Wisdom for Building Community; Editors Kosha Anja Joubert, Robin Alfred; Permanent Publications, 2007.

Coming Back to Life – Practices to Reconnect Our Lives, Our World; Joanna Macy, Molly Young Brown; New Society Publishers, 1999.

Corepower: Leadership from Your Core; Baud Vandenbemden, Lien De Coster; Createspace publishing, 2014.

Coyote's Guide to Connecting with Nature; Jon Young, Ellen Haas, Evan McGown; Owlink Media, 2010.

Find Your Power – A Toolkit for Resilience and Positive Change; Chris Johnstone; Permanent Publications, 2nd Edition, 2010.

Food Not Lawns – How to Turn Your Yard into a Garden and Your Neighbourhood into a Community; H.C. Flores; Chelsea Green, 2006.

Group Works: A Pattern Language for Bringing Life to Meetings and Other Gatherings; Group Pattern Language Project, 2011.

People & Permaculture – Caring and Designing for Ourselves, Each Other and the Planet; Looby Macnamara; Permanent Publications, 2012.

Permaculture Principles and Pathways Beyond Sustainability; David Holmgren; Permanent Publications, 2002.

Reconnecting with Nature – Finding Wellness Through Restoring Your Bond with the Earth; Michael J. Cohen; Ecopress, 1997.

Stories of the Great Turning; Editors Peter Reason and Melanie Newman; Vala Publishing Co-operative, 2013.

Systems Thinking Playbook; Linda Booth Sweeney, Dennis Meadows; Chelsea Green Publishing, 2010.

The Earthpath – Grounding Your Spirit in the Rhythms of Nature; Starhawk; Harperone, 2004.

The Empowerment Manual – A Guide for Collaborative Groups; Starhawk; New Society Publishers, 2011.

The Hidden Messages in Water; Dr Masaru Emoto; Artria books, 2001.

The Holistic Life – Sustainability Through Permaculture; Ian Lillington; Axion Publishing, 2007.

The Power of Just Doing Stuff – How Local Action Can Change the World; Rob Hopkins; Green Books, 2013.

The Seven Habits of Highly Effective People – Powerful Lessons in Personal Change; Steven Covey; Simon and Schuster, 1989.

Think! Before It's Too Late; Edward De Bono; Vermilion, 2009.

Thinking in Systems – A Primer; Donella Meadows; Chelsea Green, 2008.

We Are the Ones We've Been Waiting For – Light in a Time of Darkness; Alice Walker; Weidenfeld and Nicolson, 2007.

You Are Therefore I Am – A Declaration of Dependence; Satish Kumar; Green Books, 2002.

Websites

Blog: www.loobymacnamara.com

Fair trade business: www.spiralsofabundance.com

Courses: www.designedvisions.com

People and permaculture facilitators: www.thrivingways.org

Permaculture Association Britain: www.permaculture.org.uk

Permaculture magazine: www.permaculture.co.uk

The Work That Reconnects network: http://workthatreconnects.org

Transition Network: www.transitionnetwork.org

Biomimicry library of strategies: www.asknature.org

Films

Anima Mundi; Peter Charles Downey; United Natures, 2011.

Celebrating What's Right With the World; www.celebratewhatsright.com/film

Occupy Love; Velcrow Ripper; Fierce Love, 2013.

The Growing Edge; Donna Read & Starhawk; Belili Productions.

Global Gardener; Bill Mollison; Bullfrog Films.

The Story of Stuff; http://storyofstuff.org/

The Story of Solutions; http://storyofstuff.org/movies/the-story-of-solutions/

Numen; www.numenfilm.com

TED talks; www.ted.com

References

1 *Coming Back to Life – Practices to Reconnect Our Lives, Our World*; Joanna Macy and Molly Young Brown; New Society Publishers, 1998.

2 *Systems Thinking Playbook*; Linda Booth Sweeney and Dennis Meadows; Chelsea Green Publishing, 2010, p140.

3 Cited in *Greenspirit* magazine, volume 16:1, 2014, p10.

4 *Active Hope – How to Face the Mess We're in Without Going Crazy*; Joanna Macy and Chris Johnstone; New World Library, 2012, p148.

5 *The Fifth Sacred Thing*; Starhawk; Bantam books, 1993, p153.

6 *The Hidden Messages in Water*; Dr Masaru Emoto; Artria books, 2001.

7 *Buddhist Boot Camp*; Timber Hawkeye; Harper One, 2013, pxiii.

8 Cited in *Permaculture* magazine, issue no.68.

9 *Celebrate What's Right with the World* film; Dewitt Jones; www.celebratewhatsright.com/film

10 see www.resilience.org/stories/2005-04-01/why-our-food-so-dependent-oil

11 see www.no-tar-sands.org/what-are-the-tar-sands/

12 *Earth Pilgrim*; Satish Kumar; Green Books, 2009, p105.

13 Cited in *The Soul of Leadership*; Deepak Chopra; Rider Random House, 2010, p143.

14 *Active Hope – How to Face the Mess We're in Without Going Crazy*; Joanna Macy and Chris Johnstone; New World Library, 2012, p13-28.

15 *Active Hope – How to Face the Mess We're in Without Going Crazy*; Joanna Macy and Chris Johnstone; New World Library, 2012, p17.

16 *The Power of Just Doing Stuff*; Rob Hopkins; Green Books, 2013, p67.

17 *The Seven Habits of Highly Effective People – Powerful Lessons in Personal Change*; Steven Covey; Simon And Schuster, 1989.

18 *Earth Pilgrim*; Satish Kumar; Green Books, 2009.

19 *Billions and Billions: Thoughts on Life and Death at the Brink of the Millenium*; Carl Sagan; Ballantine Books, 1998.

20 *Call Me By My True Names*; Thich Naht Hanh; Parallax Text, 1999, p5.

21 *Coming Back to Life – Practices to Reconnect Our Lives, Our World*; Joanna Macy and Molly Young Brown; New Society Publishers, 1998, p101.

22 *Thinking in Systems – A Primer*; Donella Meadows; Chelsea Green, 2008, p170.

23 *Thinking in Systems – A Primer*; Donella Meadows; Chelsea Green, 2008, p145-165.

24 see www.efsa.europa.eu/en/press/news/130116.htm

www.theecologist.org/News/news_analysis/1873833/frontline_online_whats_killing_our_bees.html

25 see http://bees.pan-uk.org/neonicotinoids

26 see www.independent.co.uk/environment/nature/victory-for-bees-as-european-union-bans-neonicotinoid-pesticides-blamed-for-destroying-bee-population-8595408.html

27 Biomimicry in Action; Janine Benyus; TED talk www.ted.com/talks/janine_benyus_biomimicry_in_action

28 *Reconnecting with Nature – Finding Wellness Through Restoring Your Bond with the Earth*; Michael Cohen; Ecopress, 1997, p48-49.

29 *Thinking Like a Mountain – Towards a Council of All Beings*; John Seed, Joanna Macy, Pat Fleming; New Catalyst Books, 2007.

30 *Last Child in the Woods*; Richard Louv; Atlantic books, 2010.

31 *Reconnecting with Nature – Finding Wellness Through Restoring Your Bond with the Earth*; Michael Cohen; Ecopress, 1997, p21.

32 Biomimicry in Action; Janine Benyus; TED talk www.ted. com/talks/janine_benyus_biomimicry_in_action

33 *Coyote's Guide to Connecting with Nature*; Jon Young, Ellen Haas, Evan McGown; Owlink Media, 2010, p41.

34 Cited in *Greenspirit* magazine, volume 16:1, 2014, p12.

35 *Blessed Unrest*; Paul Hawken; Penguin books, 2008, p4.

36 *Blessed Unrest*; Paul Hawken; Penguin books, 2008, p163.

37 *The Seven Habits of Highly Effective People – Powerful Lessons In Personal Change*; Steven Covey; Simon And Schuster, 1989.

38 Taken from the CD with *Saved by a Poem*; Kim Rosen; Hay House, 2009.

39 *Call Me By My True Names*; Thich Naht Hanh; Parallax Text, 1999, p150.

40 *The Hidden Messages in Water*; Dr Masaru Emoto; Artria books, 2001, pxxii.

41 *The Soul of Leadership*; Deepak Chopra; Rider Random House, 2010, p87.

42 *Find Your Power – A Toolkit for Resilience and Positive Change*; Chris Johnstone; Permanent Publications, 2nd Edition, 2010, p81.

43 *Facilitating with Heart*; Lasley; Lulu Press, 2010, p108.

44 *Juicy Pens, Thirsty Paper*; SARK; Three Rivers Press, 2008.

45 *Thinking in Systems – A Primer*; Donella Meadows; Chelsea Green, 2008, p163-164.

46 *The Hidden Messages in Water*; Dr Masaru Emoto; Artria books, 2001, pxxii.

Enjoyed this book?

SUBSCRIBE
to *the*
sustainable living magazine

Permaculture magazine offers tried and tested ways of creating flexible, low cost approaches to sustainable living

BE INSPIRED by practical solutions and ideas

SAVE on our exclusive subscriber offers

FREE home delivery – never miss an issue

HELP US SUPPORT permaculture projects

in places with no access to currency

SUBSCRIBE, CHECK OUR DAILY UPDATES
AND JOIN THE PERMACULTURE ENEWSLETTER TO RECEIVE SPECIAL
OFFERS ON NEW AND EXISTING BOOKS, TOOLS AND PRODUCTS:

www.permaculture.co.uk